off the wall

The publishers gratefully acknowledge the financial
assistance of the Arts Council/An Chomhairle Ealaíon

First published in 2002 by Marino Books
16 Hume Street Dublin 2
Tel: (01) 661 5299; Fax: (01) 661 8583
E-mail: books@marino.ie
An imprint of Mercier Press
www.mercierpress.ie

Trade enquiries to CMD Distribution
55A Spruce Avenue
Stillorgan Industrial Park
Blackrock County Dublin
Tel: (01) 294 2560; Fax: (01) 294 2565
E.mail: cmd@columba.ie

Introduction and biographical material
© Niall MacMonagle 2002
The copyright permissions pages are
an extension of this copyright notice.

ISBN 1 86023 002 4
10 9 8 7 6 5 4 3 2 1

A CIP record for this title is available
from the British Library

Cover design by Marino Design
Cover illustration by James Hanley
Back cover photograph by Riona
MacMonagle
Printed in Ireland by ColourBooks,
Baldoyle Industrial Estate, Dublin 13

This book is sold subject to the
condition that it shall not, by way of
trade or otherwise, be lent, resold,
hired out or otherwise circulated
without the publisher's prior consent
in any form of binding or cover other
than that in which it is published and
without a similar condition including
this condition being imposed on the
subsequent purchaser.
No part of this publication may be
reproduced or transmitted in any
form or by any means, electronic or
mechanical, including photocopying,
recording or any information or
retrieval system, without the prior
permission of the publisher in writing.

Withdrawn From Stock
Dublin City Public Libraries

off the wall

edited by
Niall MacMonagle

Withdrawn From Stock
Dublin City Public Libraries

CONTENTS

for Philip, John, Riona and David

for Jeroen Olthof and Pat Palmer

Leabharlann Shráid Chaoimhín
Kevin Street Library
Tel: 01 222 8488

INTRODUCTION

'World is crazier and more of it than we think . . . '
LOUIS MACNEICE

Some poems affirm, some enrich, some console. The poems in this book are odd, unsettling, edgy, nervous, anarchic, quirky, irreverent, outrageous, bad-mannered and wacky. They speak up and speak out, confirming that life can be crazy, our way of looking at it even crazier.

In 'Danse Russe' William Carlos Williams dances 'naked, grotesquely' before his mirror in his sleeping house and becomes 'the happy genius' of his household. Tom Wayman, in love, finds himself in bed not only with his girlfriend but with Doktor Marx and Doktor Freud. Lavinia Greenlaw's 'The Gift' tells of how a nineteenth-century doctor creates the miracle of life in an unsuspecting Quaker merchant's wife. Aidan Mathews in 'Decency' lives, learns, and casts a cold and truthful eye on baby and granny, both in nappies. The bookie in Seamus Heaney's 'Among the Whins' tells

> the tale of his own dud racehorse,
> How he insured it first and then one night
> Hunted it over the edge of a quarryhole.

Waywardness has its dangers but it also has its thrills and attractions. We can so easily identify with that urge to stray from the straight and narrow. Julie O'Callaghan's 'So long chumps' strikes a chord. Mary O'Donoghue's witches make

Leabharlanna Poiblí Chathair Baile Átha Cliath
Dublin City Public Libraries
11

the break and vroom round County Clare in their 'did-it-ourselves camper van':

> We play poker, eat rose-hips and grow
> Haggedy in this place of rocks and bones

A different kind of journey turns nightmare in Robin Robertson's 'Anxiety #5' and in August Kleinzahler's 'Green Sees Things in Waves', his friend Green, having eaten 'quite a pile of acid one time', ends up with blown wiring 'behind his headlights'. Darker and more shocking is Rosita Boland's 'Lipstick'. Here the speaker, while slicing red peppers in her kitchen, hears that when Iranian revolutionary guards

> discovered women wearing lipstick
> They razor-bladed it off,
> Replacing one red gash with another

The poem, with a single frightening, unsettling image, captures more in a few lines than columns of newsprint.

Then there's the whoosh of Caitríona O'Reilly's carefree, six-year-old self when she remembers:

> The blond medallions of the aspen
> shook and burned on the first day
>
> of summer. I wore my gingham pinny
> and no knickers and waved wildly
>
> at the boats rounding the bay,
> snagging the waters to a silver V

and it's difficult to think of that cabinet table without remembering Paul Durcan's Alice Gunn, 'a cleaner woman / Down at Government Buildings' who

> got one of the security men
> To lie down on the Cabinet Table,
> And what she didn't do to him –
> And what she did do to him –
> She didn't half tell us;
> But she told us enough to be going on with

One moment a poem is talking dirty on the telephone, or falling down a hippo's throat. Next, it's on its belly and feeling dizzy as it looks down on the space beneath Dún Aengus and the 'marbling sea'; then it's at the world jigsaw final, or has Emily Brontë cleaning her car while 'water sloshes over her old trainers'.

It may seem that between the covers of this collection 'crazy, crazy is now showing everywhere' but, as Kazantzakis reminds us in *Zorba the Greek*, we all need a little madness. And at times, as in Gregory Corso's poem 'The Whole Mess . . . Almost' the only answer is 'Out the window with the window'.

NIALL MACMONAGLE

Walking Across the Atlantic

I wait for the holiday crowd to clear the beach
before stepping onto the first wave.

Soon I am walking across the Atlantic
thinking about Spain,
checking for whales, waterspouts.

I feel the water holding up my shifting weight.
Tonight I will sleep on its rocking surface.

But for now I try to imagine what
this must look like to the fish below,
the bottoms of my feet appearing, disappearing.

Billy Collins

THE WHOLE MESS . . . ALMOST

I ran up six flights of stairs
to my small furnished room
opened the window
and began throwing out
those things most important in life

First to go, Truth, squealing like a fink:
'Don't! I'll tell awful things about you!'
'Oh yeah? Well, I've nothing to hide . . . OUT!'
Then went God, glowering & whimpering in amazement:
'It's not my fault! I'm not the cause of it all!' 'OUT!'
Then Love, cooing bribes: 'You'll never know impotency!
All the girls on *Vogue* covers, all yours!'
I pushed her fat ass out and screamed:
'You always end up a bummer!'
I picked up Faith Hope Charity
all three clinging together:
'Without us you'll surely die!'
'With you I'm going nuts! Goodbye!'

Then Beauty . . . ah, Beauty —
As I led her to the window
I told her: 'You I loved best in life
. . . but you're a killer; Beauty kills!'
Not really meaning to drop her
I immediately ran downstairs
getting there just in time to catch her
'You saved me!' she cried
I put her down and told her: 'Move on.'

Went back up those six flights
went to the money
there was no money to throw out.
The only thing left in the room was Death
hiding beneath the kitchen sink:
'I'm not real!' it cried
'I'm just a rumour spread by life . . . '
Laughing I threw it out, kitchen sink and all
and suddenly realised Humour
was all that was left —
All I could do with Humour was to say:
'Out the window with the window!'

GREGORY CORSO

The Gift of Life

Dr William Pancoast, Philadelphia, 1884

In March I inseminated the wife
of a Quaker merchant who was childless.
Extensive tests had led me to believe
that the cause of her infertility lay
in the merchant's limited production of sperm.
His wife was brought to the hospital
for a final examination during which
chloroform was applied to the face and mouth.
This led to complete unconsciousness
facilitating the insertion of a speculum
and the dilation of the uterine canal.
My finest student provided the sample,
applied with the aid of a rubber syringe
commonly used for agriculture livestock.
I also took the additional precaution
of plugging the cervix with cotton rag.
It is now the day after Christmas.
I heard this morning the merchant has been
blessed with a son. God's will be done.

Lavinia Greenlaw

DANSE RUSSE

If when my wife is sleeping
and the baby and Kathleen
are sleeping
and the sun is a flame-white disc
in silken mists
above shining trees, —
if I in my north room
dance naked, grotesquely
before my mirror
waving my shirt round my head
and singing softly to myself:
'I am lonely, lonely.
I was born to be lonely,
I am best so!'
If I admire my arms, my face,
my shoulders, flanks, buttocks
against the yellow drawn shades, —

Who shall say I am not
the happy genius of my household?

WILLIAM CARLOS WILLIAMS

MARKS

My husband gives me an A
for last night's supper,
an incomplete for my ironing,
a B plus in bed.
My son says I am average,
an average mother, but if
I put my mind to it
I could improve.
My daughter believes
in Pass / Fail and tells me
I pass. Wait 'til they learn
I'm dropping out.

LINDA PASTAN

ADIOS

You shoulda seen
what a lump on a log I was.
I was the certified chauffeur
for all the family.
Dolly has piano lessons?
Dad'll drive you.
My wife is goin' to the Jewel Food Store?
Get old drippo to sit behind the wheel.
But it was more than that.
There were these eight people
all grabbing my dough
on a Friday night;
eight mouths waiting for Hamburger Helper,
and after I'd bought them
their Dream Whip
and their Keds gym shoes
they start calling me a square.
I was corny they said.
My daughter called me a male chauvinist pig
cuz I was enjoying the half-time entertainment
with the Dallas Cowboys' cheerleaders
kicking up their heels.
This is a gyp, I told myself.
I can't even relax
during a crummy football game.
I got my car keys
and headed for sunny Florida.
So long chumps.

JULIE O'CALLAGHAN

[MAY I FEEL SAID HE]

may i feel said he
(i'll squeal said she
just once said he)
it's fun said she

(may i touch said he
how much said she
a lot said he)
why not said she

(let's go said he
not too far said she
what's too far said he
where you are said she)

may i stay said he
(which way said she
like this said he
if you kiss said she

may i move said he
is it love said she)
if you're willing said he
(but you're killing said she

but it's life said he
but your wife said she
now said he)
ow said she

(tiptop said he
don't stop said she
oh no said he
go slow said she

(cccome?said he
ummm said she)
you're divine! said he
(you are Mine said she)

E. E. CUMMINGS

FAN

'Sign dese buuks, ya little bastard,
    ya'd never know
        when I'd make a killin'
            outa ya!'

BRENDAN KENNELLY

WAYMAN IN LOVE

At last Wayman gets the girl into bed.
He is locked in one of those embraces
so passionate his left arm is asleep
when suddenly he is bumped in the back.
'Excuse me,' a voice mutters, thick with German.
Wayman and the girl sit up astounded
as a furry gentleman in boots and a frock coat
climbs in under the covers.

'My name is Doktor Marx,' the intruder announces
settling his neck comfortably on the pillow.
'I'm here to consider for you the cost of a kiss.'
He pulls out a notepad. 'Let's see now,
we have the price of the mattress, this room must be rented,
your time off work, groceries for two,
medical fees in case of accidents . . . '

'Look,' Wayman says,
'couldn't we do this later?'
The philosopher sighs, and continues: 'You are affected too,
        Miss.
If you are not working, you are going to resent
your dependent position. This will influence
I assure you, your most intimate moments . . . '

'Doctor, please,' Wayman says. 'All we want
is to be left alone.'
But another beard, more nattily dressed,
is also getting into the bed.
There is a shifting and heaving of bodies
as everyone wriggles out room for themselves.

'I want you to meet a friend from Vienna,'
Marx says. 'This is Doktor Freud.'

The newcomer straightens his glasses,
peers at Wayman and the girl.
'I can see,' he begins,
'that you two have problems.'

Tom Wayman

The Video

When Laura was born, Ceri watched.
They all gathered around Mum's bed —
Dad and the midwife and Mum's sister
and Ceri. 'Move over a bit,' Dad said —
he was trying to focus the camcorder
on Mum's legs and the baby's head.

After she had a little sister,
and Mum had gone back to being thin,
and was twice as busy, Ceri played
the video again and again.
She watched Laura come out, and then,
in reverse, she made her go back in.

Fleur Adcock

AN EXECUTION REMEMBERED

A decapitated chicken bolted
across the yard, scattering gouts
from its blunt neck. the blood seeped
between my closed lids and even
into the sun which returned it

in a fine spray, making rubies
of dull stones. the bird convulsed,
sternum jerked on the earth, back and forth,
punctual as a pendulum; metronome
for the rhythmic pace of the butcheress

with the bright axe. since then she died,
dignified as a headless pullet.
the sun makes scarlet stained-glass
of my eyelids, still throbbing
like an ubiquitous metronome.

TREVOR JOYCE

THE CABINET TABLE

Alice Gunn is a cleaner woman
Down at Government Buildings,
And after seven o'clock Mass last night
(Isn't it a treat to be able to go to Sunday Mass
On a Saturday! To sit down to Saturday Night TV
Knowing you've fulfilled your Sunday obligation!)
She came back over to The Flats for a cup of tea
(I offered her sherry but she declined –
Oh, I never touch sherry on a Saturday night –
Whatever she meant by that, I don't know).
She had us all in stitches, telling us
How one afternoon after a Cabinet Meeting
She got one of the security men
To lie down on the Cabinet Table,
And what she didn't do to him –
And what she did do to him –
She didn't half tell us;
But she told us enough to be going on with.
'Do you know what it is?' she says to me:
'No,' says I, 'what is it?'
'It's mahogany,' she says, 'pure mahogany.'

PAUL DURCAN

Nineteen Eighty-Four

Saint Laurence O'Toole meant business
with his high cheekbones and stiff mitre.
Mary wore lipstick and no shoes
so I sat on her side of the altar.

She wasn't frightening at all
as with her halo at a rakish angle,
she trod on plaster clouds and stars
behind a row of five pence candles.

She always appeared ignorant
of her swelling middle, or
even politely averted her eyes
(and she never got any bigger).

Later on I couldn't look
for fear she might suddenly move.
That year whole crowds of Marys
wept bloody tears in their groves,

making signs with fragmented hands.
And I knew or guessed why –
the worst thing a schoolgirl could do
was to give birth alone and die

under Mary's hapless supervision.
No apparitions in grottoes
or wingèd babies with cradle-cap
for the likes of those.

Caitríona O'Reilly

DECENCY

Inter faeces et urinam nascimur – Augustine

Granny's smoking in her sickroom
On the left-hand side of the landing.
Life goes so fast. She can't draw breath.
If I knock at her door she'll be squatting
On a Jumbo bale of geriatric diapers.

On the right-hand side of the landing,
The lovely scent of my daughter's urine.
I butter her vulva with cold cream,
Her scorched anus, her dimply bum,
And I parcel her into a sellotaped Pampers.

In the middle, straight before me,
At eye-level, my level, a tacked crucifix.
Jesus in a loincloth on the cross.
What I wondered at twelve and thirteen was:
Were they ashamed to show his cock?

Had his cadaver a hard-on?
Was the Church ashamed he'd been docked,
A Jew of the House of Jacob,
Or was it, as the Schoolmen stated,
That the Lord had never defecated?

You live. You learn. Life goes so fast.
Whether swaddling clothes in a stable
Or a linen sheet in a tomb,
There are things so holy they should be hidden –
Those parts of the body that, moistening,

Disclose most fully the flesh and blood
Which haunts us more than metaphysics.
It is our own species we eat and drink;
And the odour of sanctity on my hands –
Shit and piss – is a relic of decency.

AIDAN MATHEWS

HITCHER

I'd been tired, under
the weather, but the ansaphone kept screaming:
One more sick-note, mister, and you're finished. Fired.
I thumbed a lift to where the car was parked.
A Vauxhall Astra. It was hired.

I picked him up in Leeds.
He was following the sun to west from east
with just a toothbrush and the good earth for a bed. The
      truth,
he said, was blowin' in the wind,
or round the next bend.

I let him have it
on the top road out of Harrogate – once
with the head, then six times with the Krooklok
in the face – and didn't even swerve.
I dropped it into third

and leant across
to let him out, and saw him in the mirror
bouncing off the kerb, then disappearing down the verge.
We were the same age, give or take a week.
He'd said he liked the breeze

to run its fingers
through his hair. It was twelve noon.
The outlook for the day was moderate to fair.
Stitch that, I remember thinking,
you can walk from there.

SIMON ARMITAGE

Among the Whins

Wasps in foxgloves. And the three walkers
Faltered on the brae. The hot ditches
Shadowed them, the steep incline took them
From one another into themselves
And on into the mood of confidences –
Accountant, vet and bookie, among the whins.
They stopped of one accord but did not speak
(The lark unstoppable over their heads).
Who is going to tell? The vet remembers
A reeking horse-box at a point-to-point,
Guiding his partner's wife in there for shelter
As the crowd starts a big rush for the cars
At the end of the meet. Ancient rain
Drums on the roof above them. Suddenly
He hauls on the taut oiled wires and a door
Half-rises and hangs there, darkening them.
He turns, rubbing his hands under his arms,
To take hold of the small cleft of her back
And smell deliberately at her perfumed neck,
So tender to his half-shaved underlip.
They are roused inside a second but then stop
Without speaking once and manage out
Into the crowd still hurrying through the mud,
To separate naturally and arrive
Hot and bothered with their soaked, half-gathered
Families, asking, 'Where's so and so?' And each
Gets settled, rubbing the windscreen, peering.
This is the vet's story he must tell
So the other two can begin on theirs.
Errigal stands guard on the horizon
And everything is going on as usual.

For example, when the bookie's compliments
Have been expressed – 'Aren't you the right cute whore!' –
He starts on the tale of his own dud racehorse,
How he insured it first and then one night
Hunted it over the edge of a quarryhole.
And now it's the vet's partner, rattling into shot
In an old pick-up, slowing down and shouting,
'Haven't some bastards the greatest times of all!'
And now it's the accountant: 'That reminds me . . .'

SEAMUS HEANEY

SONG

My love got in the car
And sat on my banana,
My unobserved banana
And my organic crisps.

We spoke of life and love,
His rump on my banana,
My hidden, soft banana
And my forgotten crisps.

He kissed me more than once
As he sat on that banana,
That newly-squashed banana
And those endangered crisps.

We looked up at the stars –
Beneath him, my banana,
My saved-from-lunch banana
And my delicious crisps.

At last I dropped him off
And noticed the banana –
Alas, a ruined banana
And sadly damaged crisps.

You'd think he would have felt
A fairly large banana
And, if not the banana,
The lumpy bag of crisps.

But he's the kind of man
Who'll sit on a banana
For hours. Watch your banana
And guard your bag of crisps.

He waved goodbye and smiled,
Benign as a banana.
'I love you, daft banana,'
Said I, and ate the crisps.

WENDY COPE

Toilet

I wonder will I speak to the girl
sitting opposite me on this train.
I wonder will my mouth open and say,
'Are you going all the way
to Newcastle?' or 'Can I get you a coffee?'
Or will it simply go 'aaaaah'
as if it had a mind of its own?

Half closing eggshell blue eyes,
she runs her hand through her hair
so that it clings to the carriage cloth,
then slowly frees itself.
She finds a brush and her long fair hair
flies back and forth like an African fly-whisk,
making me feel dizzy.

Suddenly, without warning,
she packs it all away in a rubber band
because I have forgotten to look out
the window for a moment.
A coffee is granted permission
to pass between her lips
and does so eagerly, without fuss.

A tunnel finds us looking out the window
into one another's eyes. She leaves her seat,
but I know that she likes me
because the light saying 'TOILET'
has come on, a sign that she is lifting
her skirt, taking down her pants
and peeing all over my face.

Hugo Williams

GREEN LIGHT AND GAMMA RAYS

Miss Liberty is green, the horizon and sky
plus yellow skin.

> She is a minority too, colour
> of ridiculous Martian fable
> and not a man.

Handicapped, disabled.
Another immigrant.

THYLIAS MOSS

ANXIETY # 5

I need to go to the bathroom. Inside it is very bright, with spotless white tiles from floor to ceiling. As I am washing my hands, I notice the door of the shower is covered in pieces of coloured paper. Crossing the room, I see that these are Polaroids, taped neatly in rows. They show a man going through the stages of torture with a razor blade, his mouth held shut with the same duct-tape used to display the photographs; the interior, visible behind him, clearly the same bathroom.

The process had been drawn out over some time: a number of the wounds had already congealed. The lines were very straight – across the face and chest, around the arms, and so on – like the lines on graph-paper. In the first photo you can see his eyes. By the end he is unrecognisable. The last photograph is blurred.

There is no sign of blood on the white tiles; they are clean and fresh. I return to the Polaroids and notice the last one is not blurred any more, it is still developing. I begin to make out the back of a man's head. He is looking at pieces of coloured paper.

ROBIN ROBERTSON

ONE MINUTE WITH EILEEN

1

After finishing work
I take a shortcut through Soho

and pass an open door
that says: two pounds

for one minute with Eileen.
Well, I ponder this,

then turn and turn about.
The old lady behind the counter

gives me a blue ticket.
Sit there, she says, Eileen

is occupied at present.
I'll wait on the street, I say.

2

So I took a turn or two
through the Chinese,

like a man about
business in the town,

and soon enough, a youth
doused in gel emerges

head-down
like a duck in thunder

and high-tailed it
in a north-easterly,

and the lady waved me in.
The inside door opened and

I sit in an armchair
facing Eileen.

3

Now, she explains,
I'm a tipsy girl.

If you want to touch me,
that's twenty; if you want me

to touch you, that's forty.
Full sex is sixty.

Anything after that
is over a hundred.

And what, I asked,
do I get for my two pound?

You get to hear the prices, she said.

DERMOT HEALY

HOLDING PATTERN, DÚN AENGUS

At the edge, safe on your belly,
you relish the whole island tilting

its dark grey wing. Below you
seabirds patrolling their levels,

above you a lichen-bright butterfly
haloing crookedly. Your face

is washed by those updrafts, the breath
of a marbling sea. Hang in there

shaken free
at ease in the swim of air.

MARK GRANIER

Why I Am Not a Painter

I am not a painter, I am a poet.
Why? I think I would rather be
a painter, but I am not. Well,

for instance, Mike Goldberg
is starting a painting. I drop in.
'Sit down and have a drink' he
says. I drink; we drink. I look
up. 'You have SARDINES in it.'
'Yes, it needed something there.'
'Oh.' I go and the days go by
and I drop in again. The painting
is going on, and I go, and the days
go by. I drop in. The painting is
finished. 'Where's SARDINES?'
All that's left is just
letters, 'It was too much,' Mike says.

But me? One day I am thinking of
a colour: orange. I write a line
about orange. Pretty soon it is a
whole page of words, not lines.
Then another page. There should be
so much more, not of orange, of
words, of how terrible orange is
and life. Days go by. It is even in
prose, I am a real poet. My poem
is finished and I haven't mentioned
orange yet. It's twelve poems, I call
it ORANGES. And one day in a gallery
I see Mike's painting, called SARDINES.

FRANK O'HARA

'MADAM'

Madam
I have sold you
an electric plug
an electric torch
an electric blanket
an electric bell
an electric cooker
an electric kettle
an electric fan
an electric iron
an electric drier
an electric mixer
an electric washer
an electric knife
an electric clock
an electric fire
an electric toothbrush
an electric razor
an electric teapot
an electric eye
and electric light.
Allow me to sell you
an electric chair.

CHRISTOPHER LOGUE

GREEN SEES THINGS IN WAVES

Green first thing each day sees waves –
the chair, armoire, overhead fixtures, you name it,
waves – which, you might say, things really are,
but Green just lies there awhile breathing
long slow breaths, in and out, through his mouth
like he was maybe seasick, until in an hour or so
the waves simmer down and then the trails and colours
off of things, that all quiets down as well and Green
starts to think of washing up, breakfast even
with everything still moving around, colours, trails,
and sounds, from the street and plumbing next door,
vibrating – of course you might say that's what
sound really is, after all, vibrations – but Green,
he's not thinking physics at this stage, nuh-uh,
our boy's only trying to get himself out of bed,
get a grip, but sometimes, and this is the kicker,
another party, shall we say, is in the room
with Green, and Green knows this other party
and they do not get along, which understates it
quite a bit, quite a bit, and Green knows
that this other cat is an hallucination, right,
but these two have a routine that goes way back
and Green starts hollering, throwing stuff
until he's all shook up, whole day gone to hell,
bummer . . .

       Anyhow, the docs are having a look,
see if they can't dream up a cocktail,
but seems our boy ate quite a pile of acid one time,
clinical, wow, enough juice for half a block –
go go go, little Greenie – blew the wiring out
from behind his headlights and now, no matter what,
can't find the knob to turn off the show.

AUGUST KLEINZAHLER

Celia Celia

When I am sad and weary
When I think all hope has gone
When I walk along High Holborn
I think of you with nothing on

Adrian Mitchell

Ararat

It wus never a flud, they got it all rong.
It wus a heetwave. Who ever herd of a flud
in the desert? As if we wud hav minded!
We didnt pich up on that peek to keep dry
but cool. You cant imagin the heet.
It rold in like invisibal fire, like lions breth.
Never mind an eg you cud fry a stake
on a rock, and in the shade. Sandals smoked
with evry step. You had to wear 2 pairs
and even then run. Sleeping – a nitemare,
a joke. The only way to lie down wus to souse
yor bed evry our with water – warm water –
if you cud find it. Who wonts to shlep
to the well and back 6 times a nite?
For shlep I meen skip. Forget dreems.
Dreems evaporated befor they cud reech us.

We took to a cave. It wus cool as a buchers
at ferst. Cudnt beleev our luck, problem solvd,
wed wait it out. We hung blankits over the mouth

to keep out the sun. Then dusnt the erth
heet up round us like an uven. The place ternd
into a bakers. The animals started showing up,
limping, wining. The lions came ferst and purd
at the blankits. I let them in. The lady nuzzeld
my elbow, lickt my hand with that scraper-
tung of hers. She drew blud but didnt meen to
and never came back for mor. They straggeld
past our pots and rugs, curld up in the caves dark.
After that we cud hardly refuse the rest.

In they cum, 2 by 2 trew enough.
Grunts, grumbels, grones. Mones and mews,
wines and wimpers. Clucks, chirrups,
werrings, buzzes, wissals, flooting.
Piping, worbling, fluttring, droning.
Berps, farts, sies – you name it we herd it.
The cave fild with the gurgels of a milion
animal slumbers. Youd think it wudve stunk
but the mingeld odors of a milion beests
wer sweet to the nostral like a bloom of flours.
And the dung? Strange but there wus nun.

The sky ternd yellow. We stopt eeting.
The apitite dusnt do well at that heet.
We neither slept nor woke. Ime no hero
but sumthing had to be dun. So I organize
the boys. We lit a fire outside, wated til
the coles glowed then herded the lot strate out
onto them. The trick is once theyve been over
those coles the ground dusnt seem so hot.
A quick shock and you can handel anything.
Shem led the way: up the hill to the top.

We capt the peek up there like a nippal.
It wusnt exactly cool but we had a chance.
The sky wus blew agen for 1 thing.
Down below all you cud see wus yellow fog.
No ground, no hills. We hung on our iland of air.
So cleer up there, cleer as a shaving mirrer.
You hav a good long look at yorself
at a time like that. I didnt like wot I saw:
greed and mor greed. Iternal disatisfaction.
Therst does funny things to you.
I even wept. I had no teers of corse
but I felt the rivulets of dust on my cheek
like guttermarks on brick. I felt rite to weep.

Its trew a duv flew up to us. A speck
shivring in the haze below, it flapt itself
into shape like a mirage cuming up
from the fog. It lit on my sholder,
put its beek to my eer to whisper sumthing –
the sweetest message ever herd.
Tho I cudnt make it out at ferst,
not until I put my finger in my eer.
I drew it out cool, damp: a drop of water
bellying on the end of it. I tried to shout
the news but my throte wudnt make a sound.

The ferst drops steemd, sizzeld and stung.
By then I didnt no if any 1 in the sprall
of flesh wus alive still. But as the rain fell
I herd mones and yelps all round, a crazy
dog barkt up at the thunderheds
in a rage, a fox howled, the frogs flooted
like an organ. Necks rose like plant stems.

Wite clouds bloomd up from the yellow fog.
I cried wen I saw them. I new we had wun.
Thats the trooth. I never got my voice back
so I cudnt put rite the talk of fluds.
Not until I lernt pen and ink. And I wus
sixty when it happen not 6 hundred.
If I liv to 2 hundred Ile be happy. A drop
just fell on my page. I luv the rain, who dusnt.
Anuther drop. Like littal berries, spattrings
of juice were they hit my ink. I let them be.
Be the teers I cudnt cry. The Lords dew.

Henry Shukman

The Tortoise

The tortoise goes movey, movey.

Anonymous

ZANY RAIN

'He started talking dirty to me on the phone.
I felt silly, trembling all over,
he talked like I'd never heard him talk before,
I was shaking, shaking, and then my God
I had this orgasm in that quiet office,
by myself, alone,
and as I came and came
his low sweet mocking laughter
fell all over me
like zany rain
on the dimpled river.'

BRENDAN KENNELLY

MESSAGE

Jill. Fred phoned. He can't make tonight.
He said he'd call again, as soon as poss.
I said (on your behalf) OK, no sweat.
He said to tell you he was fine,
Only the crap, he said, you know, it sticks,
The crap you have to fight.
You're sometimes nothing but a walking shithouse.

I was well acquainted with the pong myself,
I told him, and I counselled calm.
Don't let the fuckers get you down,
Take the lid off the kettle a couple of minutes,
Go on the town, burn someone to death,
Find another tart, give her some hammer,
Live while you're young, until it palls,
Kick the first blind man you meet in the balls.

Anyway he'll call again.

I'll be back in time for tea.

Your loving mother.

HAROLD PINTER

The Video Box: 25

If you ask what my favourite programme is
it has to be that strange world jigsaw final.
After the winner had defeated all his rivals
with harder and harder jigsaws, he had to prove his mettle
by completing one last absolute mindcrusher
on his own, under the cameras, in less than a week.
We saw, but he did not, what the picture would be:
the mid-Atlantic, photographed from a plane,
as featureless a stretch as could be found,
no weeds, no flotsam, no birds, no oil, no ships,
the surface neither stormy nor calm, but ordinary,
a light wind on a slowly rolling swell.
Hand-cut by a fiendish jigger to simulate,
but not to have, identical beaks and bays,
it seemed impossible; but the candidate –
he said he was a stateless person, called himself Smith –
was impressive: small, dark, nimble, self-contained.
The thousands of little grey tortoises were scattered
on the floor of the studio; we saw the clock; he started.
His food was brought to him, but he hardly ate.
He had a bed, with the light only dimmed to a weird blue,
never out. By the first day he had established
the edges, saw the picture was three metres long
and appeared to represent (dear God!) the sea.
Well, it was a man's life, and the silence
(broken only by sighs, click of wood, plop of coffee
in paper cups) that kept me fascinated.
Even when one hand was picking the edge-pieces
I noticed his other hand was massing sets
of distinguishing ripples or darker cross-hatching or
incipient wave-crests; his mind,

if not his face, worked like a sea.
It was when he suddenly rose from his bed
at two, on the third night, went straight over
to one piece and slotted it into a growing central patch,
then back to bed, that I knew he would make it.
On the sixth day he looked haggard and slow,
with perhaps a hundred pieces left,
of the most dreary unmarked lifeless grey.
The camera showed the clock more frequently.
He roused himself, and in a quickening burst
of activity, with many false starts, began
to press that inhuman insolent remnant together.
He did it, on the evening of the sixth day.
People streamed onto the set. Bands played.
That was fine. But what I liked best
was the last shot of the completed sea,
filling the screen; then the saw-lines disappeared,
till almost imperceptibly the surface moved
and it was again the real Atlantic, glad
to distraction to be released, raised
above itself in growing gusts, allowed
to roar as rain drove down and darkened,
allowed to blot, for a moment, the orderer's hand.

Edwin Morgan

COUPLING

On the wall above the bedside lamp
a large crane-fly is jump-starting
a smaller crane-fly – or vice versa.
They do it tail to tail, like Volkswagens:
their engines must be in their rears.

It looks easy enough. Let's try it.

FLEUR ADCOCK

WHAT I SAW

The man who lives on the left side of us
just tiptoed through our backyard
carrying a stick with a pair of pantyhose
waving on the top like a banner.
He climbed into the backyard of the people
who live on our right and lowered
the unmentionables onto the clothesline,
then hopped back over two fences
and was gone.

JULIE O'CALLAGHAN

THE BRIEFCASE

for Seamus Heaney

I held the briefcase at arm's length from me;
the oxblood or liver
eelskin with which it was covered
had suddenly grown supple.

I'd been waiting in line for the cross-town
bus when an almighty cloudburst
left the sidewalk a raging torrent.

And though it contained only the first
inkling of this poem, I knew I daren't
set the briefcase down
to slap my pockets for an obol –

for fear it might slink into a culvert
and strike out along the East River
for the sea. By which I mean the 'open' sea.

PAUL MULDOON

EDICT

In July 1439, a kissing prohibition
was legislated to control
the spread of the plague

I go to the cot
where death has blackened my wife
and clamp her plucking hands
between my own.
Her fingers are bulbous
blue-purple,
the nails sunk like chinks
in the stretch of flesh.
Stain from a copper ring,
the grey-green of lichen
looped round one finger.
Lumps on her neck
swell by the hour. Hens' eggs
laid under the skin
below her ears.
I wait for the cough
to clamour behind her ribs,
and bright blood slicks
her lips. I tilt for a kiss
and sip sickness,
drink the sour blight
to put me asleep with my wife.

MARY O'DONOGHUE

FINDRUM

Findrum:
the same room:
6 A.M.
10 years later, and I am
still here,
sitting in a similar
though not the same
armchair,
and not gazing
at you naked
asleep on the bed
nor waiting
but only staring
at an empty, sagging bed.

Oh for you to be here
and we could sag it more:
even break it
right down to the floor!

PEARSE HUTCHINSON

Lucky Mrs Higgins

When our mother
won a fridge
with Becker's Tea,
she got her photograph
in the *Sentinel*
shaking hands
with the man from head office.

The fridge was also
in the frame.
She wore a big wide hat
she kept on top of the wardrobe
for fridge winning days.

It went nice
with the crimplene two piece
she got for Mary Theresa's wedding.

In the photo
with the fridge
and the man from head office
she didn't look anything like herself.

Rita Ann Higgins

In School

We remembered and forgot,
We repeated, remembered and forgot,
We recited and forgot.
We chalked on slates,
We rubbed it out.
We did sums with pencils.
We dipped into inkwells,
We made letters with pen and ink,
    small letters between blue lines
    BIG LETTERS BETWEEN RED LINES.
We crossed out words,
We crossed out lines.
We soaked up blobs
    on pink blotting paper.

The school added us.
The school subtracted us.
The school multiplied us.
The school divided us.

NOEL MONAGHAN

Leabharlanna Poibli Chathair Baile Átha Cliath
Dublin City Public Libraries

The Perfect Bar of Soap

Whenever Pilate travelled on horseback
To foreign parts
He always carried in his saddlebag
The perfect bar of soap –
And you could say
That he was simply preparing
For the inevitable.

But
Whether Pilate knew
What the inevitable was
Or where it would take place
Is another matter –
And where he obtained the soap
Has always been a mystery.

Recent discoveries,
However,
Have shown quite clearly
That the soap was a product
Of the only factory in Rome
To have paid its workers
At a very high rate.

It is not surprising
Therefore
That when Pilate washed his hands
Of the Jew
He walked away
Clean
As a whistle.

Patrick Galvin

THE SHOW

A giant turd the hippo
steams on the earth. The keeper
enters her patch, sets down
a feeding bucket. Her eyes
stay closed. Onlookers wait.
He strokes the massive face,
sidles round her impassive
head, rests a hip against
her neck, leans over to
slap her cheek once.
Her eyes blink
closed but the huge jaw
drops ivory fangs
and the world is
the coral pink inside
of her mouth, yawning
tongue and palate –
the minute we see it
we are falling
down her throat.

CATHERINE PHIL MACCARTHY

The Seahorse Family

The sea horse is a question mark in the ark of the ocean
    that's carried it without question all this way.
Mythical as a unicorn and even less believable
    with its dragon head, its body a legless horse
        perpetually rearing, its monkey tail
    anchoring it to sea grass, sponge or coral,
but my love, my mate,
    no stranger than who you've become to yourself,
        feeling large as a whale and small as a human.
Today I'd have us be sea horse, and I,
    being the male, would be the one in the family way.
I'd carry our hippocamp, our capal mara, our shy sea pony,
    our question mark, anchored in you,
unquestionably unfurling its body day by tidal day.

Greg Delanty

The Bag Ladies

From Ballinahinch to
the Eastern Balkans
they talk to themselves in the streets,
they wear a look in the eye
from which everyone turns, it is
the look where the inside and the outside meet.
Now there is frost and they talk of
summers from the past, the roses.
When we are forgetful under the sun, they
talk of winters to come.
They are many
and few of them are loved and
nobody understands them.

Anne Haverty

The Masochist's Week

Moanday,
Tearsday,
Woundsday,
Fearsday,

Frightday,
Sufferday,
Stunday.

Anonymous

Seven Things Nature Did in the Last Five Minutes

1
Birdsang.

2
Rained.

3
Held speeding cars and their occupants
pretty firmly on the planet.

4
Suffered interminable noise, pollution and pain.

5
Produced interminable noise, pollution and pain.

6
Organised seal culls.

7
Smoked neurotically.

Pat Boran

THE NIGHT'S TAKINGS

for Cathal McCabe

The whores had disappeared by the time
we got there and the barman smiled,
totting up the night's takings.
So here we were, two Northern lads perched
on high stools in the middle of Europe,

the last snow black on the cobblestones,
a way down marble stairs to the seen-
it-all-before janitor, the ballroom kitted
out for ex-party types, the local mafia,
as we looked along the longest street –

the shoplights dimmed, the watchful mannequins,
the clackety-clack of the military,
the wary taxi, the metallic sky,
and the inevitable echo
that is neither here nor there.

GERALD DAWE

A SEVERED LEG

*A stretch of the Grand Union Canal in London is to be dredged
today after a severed leg wrapped in plastic was seen floating
near Regent's Park.*

The *Guardian*, 11 December 1989

This sliver of horror
Is stated matter-of-factly
At the bottom left-hand corner of page five.

Not a hundred yards from my window,
The Grand Union Canal laps sullenly,
Littered with the usual debris from Camden Market.
Even rubbish becomes more bearable when you consider
The innocence of orange peel, beer cans,
And plastic bags that are bloated with air,
Not with a decaying piece of human flesh.

I wondered all day what they have done with it.
Have they buried it
Or are they waiting to find the other bits?

Somehow, the conscious wrapping up
Of that severed limb disturbs me more than anything;
The neat and workmanlike job of murder
Being posted like a parcel
Into the uncertain depths of the canal.

And late-night radio
Goes on meandering intimately through the room,
Sending out those smooth and comforting songs
That con one into thinking at the end of the day
That everything's all right, really.

ROSITA BOLAND

BUYING A LETTERBOX

Another mouth to feed.
Our best face
turned to the world,
catching the brass
eye of the sun.

Should we buy the type
that snaps shut,
a trap scattering
bills and final reminders
like feathers, fur?

Or the limper kind
that yields easily,
tongue slobbering around
the postman's hand,
yet still eats anything,

digesting the bad news
as casually as the good?

DENNIS O'DRISCOLL

SHAKESPEAREAN

Someone I know was lolling in the doorway
of a stuffy factory office where he worked
absorbing early April UV rays
when down the yard the General Manager
came striding clad in a protective white
crisp overall against industrial grime.
The gaffer twitched an eyebrow then observed:
'I see you *like* the sun; a nice bright day?'
The idler laconically riposted:
'It is the bright day that brings forth the adder;
and that craves wary walking.' One week later
Head Office sent him his P45

PETER READING

She Elopes with Marc Chagall

Across fields of rotting cabbages
That nobody wanted to buy
The girl I loved went flying
To the other end of the sky.

Up she flew –
Over the enormous satchels
Of the homebound scholars;
Over the disused dancehalls
And empty factories;
Over the wandering dogs
In the itinerant encampments;
Over the five upturned wheelbarrows
Outside Grogan's Hardware Store
On Main Street, Swords;
Over the fleet of Escort vans
Selling fruit, fuel and vegetables
On the Dublin–Belfast road.

When I went to the doctor, he said
'In a week or two, it'll be Easter,
The sun will shine after tea,
You'll be yourself again,
Sure of who you are,
Clear as a bell,
With all the time in the world
To find someone else.
In the meantime,
Should that scalding sensation
In the pit of your stomach persist,
Try writing some verse.'

Tra-la-la, la-la.
When it's springtime in Ireland,
The fog comes in from the sea,
The birds revive in the mornings,
The earth smells sweet under me.

At night the Rockabill foghorn
Summons her back from the dead,
I remember her cheeks in blossom,
The way that she turned her head.

Easter came and went –
Despite the quack's advice,
I'm no better, now
Than when I began.
I torment myself
By chanting their names:
Maggie-Maggie,
Marc Chagall.

MICHAEL GORMAN

ON THE AMTRAK FROM BOSTON TO NEW YORK CITY

The white woman across the aisle from me says, 'Look,
look at all the history, that house
on the hill there is over two hundred years old,'
as she points out the window past me

into what she had been taught. I have learned
little more about American history during my few days
back East than what I expected and far less
of what we should all know of the tribal stories

whose architecture is 15,000 years older
than the corners of the house that sits
museumed on the hill. 'Walden Pond,'
the woman on the train asks, 'Did you see Walden Pond?'

and I don't have a cruel enough heart to break
her own by telling her there are five Walden Ponds
on my little reservation out West
and at least a hundred more surrounding Spokane,

the city I pretend to call my home. 'Listen,'
I could have told her. 'I don't give a shit
about Walden. I know the Indians were living stories
around that pond before Walden's grandparents were born

and before his grandparents' grandparents were born.
I'm tired of hearing about Don-fucking-Henley saving it, too,
because that's redundant. If Don Henley's brothers and sisters
and mothers and fathers hadn't come here in the first place

then nothing would need to be saved.'
But I didn't say a word to the woman about Walden
Pond because she smiled so much and seemed delighted
that I thought to bring her an orange juice

back from the food car. I respect elders
of every colour. All I really did was eat
my tasteless sandwich, drink my Diet Pepsi
and nod my head whenever the woman pointed out

another little piece of her country's history
while I, as all Indians have done
since this war began, made plans
for what I would do and say the next time

somebody from the enemy thought I was one of their own.

SHERMAN ALEXIE

No Weirdos Please

Sitting alone in Bewleys.
The guy at the next table
couldn't keep his eyes off me.
'Psssst,' he said
'Are you Native-Speaking
        Bi-Sexual
        Box-Number 873
who seeks help in improvising
the Kama Sutra through
the medium of Irish
No weirdos need apply?'

I shook my head.

'Not I . . . I'm middle-aged hippy
who has never had it
at 16,000 feet because
I'm scared stiff of flying.
Photo appreciated.'

'Pssst,' said the girl
behind the newspaper.
'Are you Rough Raw Randy
but very sincere Psychopath
who seeks lasting relationship
until tomorrow morning with
perverted dental receptionist
who plays the accordion
the imaginative way?'

I shook my head.

'Not today
but I'm willing to learn.'

I was secretly waiting to meet
long leggy lepidopterist
wild willing but discreet
who is into assertion training
for insects
seeks man with own supply
of spiders
and fifteen-foot extension flex.

She never did show
and so
I'm sitting alone in Bewleys
trying hard not to look
like a Box-Number.

PAT INGOLDSBY

GHOST SHIP

after Dorothy Cross

Three nights running I have been to see it,
anchored in the winter harbour, waiting,
disappearing into the dark, and reappearing.

Tonight I want to be ferried out to it,
to press my palms against its waterlines
and touch its sides before I go aboard.

I want to go below to the immaculate galley
to undo the catches of its pristine cupboards,
and slip into the private sleeping quarters

to touch the tucked neat berths of the dead,
their metal lockers filled with personal effects,
their snapshots of the living, our locks of hair;

and be rowed back home before first light
with nothing to show for my night at sea
or a word to say for myself except the feel of it

persisting beneath me, and the tips of my fingers
glowing in the darkness when I hold them up,
where I touched it, where it won't wash off.

TOM FRENCH

Painting with Sawdust

This may sound insane
but if you take the way a saw
goes ripping and tearing
through a plank of pine or larch
– pine's a softwood while larch
is hard like bone
– if you listen to a saw giving out
those barking yelpy groans
those driven shouts and moans
that're wild as a drowning pup
or raw
like a wet shammy rubbing its knuckles
on a windowpane
– if you listen to the crazy chuckles
thrown out by a saw
in the heat of its only function in life
though to be strictly accurate that jagged blade
can't ever belong to what we call life
– if you reflect on the noises this knife
– this big thrawn toothy rather tinny knife
must make
then they might be a version those chuckles
of the way couples it's said
are always going in and out
of intimacy
which means that when the saw's
dogged panting
suddenly whoops screams and stops
– *chup!*
there's a change of tune
because now that its constant whuffing

has let up
one lover or the other must take a brush
not to paint a picture but lick up
what it seems such a pity not to leave behind
or leave new and untouched
– that tiny dune
of resiny sweet crumbs.

Tom Paulin

Country Music

He is stuck in the mud of four weeks' rain
backing a tractor through a gap
to fodder beasts. They worship at an altar
of a trailer with the tailboard off,

up to their knees in a muck moraine.
They swish the thuribles of their tails, slap
incense breath on the silage psalter,
grain, torn cud; a smothered cough.

He is stuck in the mud of that profane
ritual, his hundred fathers' handicap
of squids and squalls, and asks for a hand. We falter
and spring free. Now I'm dragging water to a frozen trough,

one with them, their muttered Bollocks, Shits and Fuck its,
a cursèd yoke beneath a pair of splashing buckets.

Peter Fallon

Buy One Now

This is a new sort of Poem,
It is Biological.
It contains a special Ingredient
(Pat. pend.) which makes it different
From other brands of poem on the market.

This new Poem does the work for you.
Just drop your mind into it
And leave it to soak
While you relax with the telly
Or go out to the pub
Or (if that is what you like)
You read a novel.

It does the work for you
While (if that is what you like)
You sleep. For it is Biological
(Pat. pend.), it penetrates
Into the darkest recesses,
It removes the understains
Which it is difficult for us
Even to speak of.

Its action is so gentle
That the most delicate mind is unharmed.
This new sort of Poem
Contains an exclusive new Ingredient
(Known only to every jackass in the trade)
And can be found in practically any magazine
You care to mention.

D. J. Enright

3 A.M. IN NEW YORK

I have been standing at the edge
of this green field all night.
My hand is sticky with sugar.

The village winks; it thinks it is
the muscle of the world. The heart.
The mouth.

The horse is standing across the field, near the fence.
He doesn't come any closer,
even in the dark, or run away.

Blood memory:
fixed on vacancy:
coming back and back for a sign –

the flat of his coat,
the shut out of his eye.

JEAN VALENTINE

THE SHOUT

We went out
into the school yard together, me and the boy
whose name and face

I don't remember. We were testing the range
of the human voice:
he had to shout for all he was worth,

I had to raise an arm
from across the divide to signal back
that the sound had carried.

He called from over the park – I lifted an arm.
Out of bounds,
he yelled from the end of the road,

from the foot of the hill,
from beyond the look-out post of Fretwell's Farm –
I lifted an arm.

He left town, went on to be twenty years dead
with a gunshot hole
in the roof of his mouth, in Western Australia.

Boy with the name and face I don't remember,
you can stop shouting now, I can still hear you.

SIMON ARMITAGE

Two Scavengers in a Truck, Two Beautiful People in a Mercedes

At the stoplight waiting for the light
                              Nine A.M. downtown San Francisco
  a bright yellow garbage truck
                    with two garbagemen in red plastic blazers
    standing on the back stoop
                          one on each side hanging on
      and looking down into
                              an elegant open Mercedes
        with an elegant couple in it
The man
      in a hip three-piece linen suit
        with shoulder-length blond hair & sunglasses
The young blond woman so casually coiffed
                    with a short skirt and coloured stockings
    on the way to his architect's office

And the two scavengers up since Four A.M.
                                  grungy from their route
                on the way home
The older of the two with grey iron hair
                            and hunched back
        looking down like some
                          gargoyle Quasimodo
And the younger of the two
                        also with sunglasses & longhair
      about the same age as the Mercedes driver

And both scavengers gazing down
                              as from a great distance
            at the cool couple

as if they were watching some odourless TV ad
                        in which everything is always possible

And the very red light for an instant
                        holding all four close together
            as if anything at all were possible
                                        between them
                across that small gulf
                                    in the high seas
                                                of this democracy.

Lawrence Ferlinghetti

Watermelons

Green Buddhas
On the fruit stand.
We eat the smile
And spit out the teeth.

Charles Simic

TRAFFIC

Drawing up to the traffic lights,
the amber's blushes deepening to red,
I'm tempted with the open road in my sights

and while I've got the revs
to throttle on regardless
through the crossroads,

the traffic just let loose,
and, stepping on it, flounce
to safety – assuming those

pedestrians
don't mind. If they take
theirs, I'll take my chance . . .

*

. . . take my chance the brakes
on this machine still work. They ease
me to a halt without a squeak.

*

Let's linger a while then under the gaze
of election losers' posters, of bra-ad
nymphs exquisite in gauze

and nothing else, of Brad
Pitt and Demi Moore,
of the Dulux dog's shaggy braids.

Let's linger a while and try not to stare
at the man in the car beside us
picking his nose, smooth our hair,

look for something good (oh what's the use)
on the radio, bite a nail, or just
breathe in the diesel perfume of the 84 bus.

*

Let's watch the people filing past
and guess where they might be going,
the quick, the slow, the blind, the lost,

the students, the shoppers, the gang
of office girls off to a sandwich and
coffee for lunch, their greying

bosses to something more grand.
Let's watch the woman who pushes a trolley
stocked with whatever she's found

by the side of the road, the folly
of jaywalkers trying to dodge
the facing traffic, the carefully

hoisted leg of a dog overcome by the urge
to take a leak as it crosses the road.
My foot on the pedal releases a surge

of impatience: 'At this rate . . . '
At this rate of chewing, by rights,
your fingernail should be down to the root.

*

Rev all you like though or idle in quiet,
you're as stuck in a Merc
as you are in a Ford or a Fiat:

rage, fume, pull over and park,
but don't assume you're getting out of here
before dark.

Train yourself in how to stay put:
learn from the pedal-powered
lycra lout

briefly at ease, the horse and cart
with a fridge, a ladder,
some kids and a kitchen sink on board,

the Seat, the Saab and the Skoda
whose dodgy exhaust
makes you shudder,

the old Jag restored at great cost,
the Nissan
that's a bucket of rust,

the ice-cream van
and the empty hearse,
and somewhere in all these cars your own –

all standing their ground in one giant pause
before the handbrakes come off
and we disperse . . .

to various urgent ports of
call: to Blackrock, Greygates and Whitehall,
Valley View and Meadow Grove,

Paradise Place, Misery Hill,
Rosary Terrace, Protestant Row,
Bray Head and Curly's Hole,

affordable suburbs (showhouses on view),
a comforting hearth,
an empty house or a bedsit for two

in the Dunes, the Elms, the Gallops, the Garth,
and other assorted
ends of the earth.

Let's serve our time and take the first shortcut
to any and every place
you want, let's leave it for dead, this sordid

paralysed town, let's cut loose
to wherever a car
can go on half a tank of unleaded gas.

*

Red becomes green. Your trip starts here.

DAVID WHEATLEY

Belongings with Attitude

Says the Toaster:
'I was bought in the
Sears in Yonkers &
I'm proud to be
American made –
Slide your bagel into me.'

And the sofa answers:
'So what, pal,
I'm a Jennifer Convertible,
think of all the things
you can do on me –
Watch TV
Roll me out
Drink a cup of Earl Grey Tea.'

'No one moves to Nebraska,'
moans the air conditioner, 'and
we didn't let on where we wuz
headed for. I told a friend
I'd been sent up the river.'

Says the kitchen table bought
in the Dominican furniture place on
Vermileya St. 'You got more room
now – upstairs and downstairs.
I've always lived in apartments,
and the subway don't rumble
this house. People are so polite
I think I'm gonna go crazy.'

And a kitchen chair butts in:
'Remember me I'm the chair
you flung in the trash room.
I was rescued by the Super,
Mr Rigo, but didn't like the
smell of garlic so I chased
you down. And, Hey, I could
do with a shine and an ice-
cold *Heineken* f rom a paper
bag. Ya know what I'm sayin',
and I see ya still got that
crappy TV stand ya found
outside the co-op on
Academy St. I hear that lady
died and her stuff is all
dispersed, and I want to know
how come there ain't no live
furniture on the streets of
Omaha, Nebraska, for a citizen to
bring home? Ain't this a city?

And the old blue lazy
chair replies: 'a fire burns
this evening & our children
lean on their elbows on the
hearth seeing corn float across
prairies like waves across the sea:
eyes large as headlights, hearts
like winter squirrels' barely beating.'

Says the mangy yellow lamp to the old
blue lazy chair: 'Shut up, please,
you're beginning to sound like a

motherfuc – Oh I better not say
it since this ain't New York –
like a dang "Dairy Queen" ice-cream,
but I gotta say,
I gotta say,
gotta say,
gotta say,

I just can't bring myself to admit it . . . '

EAMONN WALL

JINGLE

To say we shelve the adverts somewhere safe
is to say the shite we put into the sea
has no bearing upon this earthly life . . .
He slipped in stuff like this while writing copy.

PAUL FARLEY

A Brief History of Your Breasts

They began as seeds
in the darkness and remained so
till conditions were propitious
then exploded
to the size of grapefruit.

Their early history's
anecdotal, virtually
unverifiable, suffice to say
by the time I came to know them
they knew what they wanted.

They'd hang over my face
their heads heavy
as huge orchids, my tongue
the hummingbird that flitted
between them. Making love

we developed an unambiguous
shorthand. 'My breasts,' you'd say,
'Remember my breasts', as if
I was in danger of flying
or floating off the edge, your breasts

the land to which I must
surely cling. Pregnant
we looked at them lots.
'Look, my breasts,' you'd say
framing them with jersey

or blouse. I noted
in a poem of the time
they were growing like fruit,
'marbled with a thin
hyacinth tracery'. At times

you stepped aside from them
altogether and they hovered
between us like holographs,
though you bore
all their weight. After the birth

they were YOURS and HIS.
Now we discussed them
the most. They were sore,
they were tender, they were full,
they were flooding; tap their tops

some morning, they're
rock hard before he suckles.
We smiled at them now
they'd become so familiar
like a couple of favourite

nieces. Once you even blushed
with pride when I unwittingly
unlocked some of their sweetness
with a serendipitous suck.
                    Space-time
curved round them

for our son, till eventually
you had to cut him free,

fraying the feeds that bound him,
one by one by one, until
'That's it,' you announced

flapping both breasts
up and down. 'The milk's all
dried up now. Gone.' And that's
as far as we've got in this
brief history of your breasts –

not an elegy but my wonder
in words. For the moment
they are two empty pails
hanging on the door of your chest,
whistling when the wind catches them.

Tom Pow

I LIKE MY OWN POEMS

I like my own poems
best.
I quote from them
from time to time
saying, 'A poet once said',
and then follow up
with a line or two
from one of my *own* poems
appropriate to the event.
How those lines sing!
All that wisdom and beauty!
Why it tickles my ass
off its spine.
'Why those lines are mine!'
I say
and Jesus, what a bang
I get out of it.

I like the *ideas* in them,
my poems;
Ideas that hit home.
They *speak* to me.
I mean, I understand
what the hell
the damn poet's
talking about.
'Why I've been there,
the same thing,' I shout,
and Christ! What a shot it is,
a shot.

And hey.
The words!
Whew!
I can hardly stand it.
Words sure do not fail
this guy, I say.
From some world
only he knows
he bangs the bong,
but I can feel it
in the wood,
in the wood of the word,
rising to its form
in the world.
'Now, you gotta be good
to do that!' I say
and damn! It just shakes
my heart,
you know!

JACK GRAPES

POEM

The eager note on my door said 'Call me,
call when you get in!' so I quickly threw
a few tangerines into my overnight bag,
straightened my eyelids and shoulders, and

headed straight for the door. It was autumn
by the time I got around the corner, oh all
unwilling to be either pertinent or bemused, but
the leaves were brighter than grass on the sidewalk!

Funny, I thought, that the lights are on this late
and the hall door open; still up at this hour, a
champion jai-alai player like himself? Oh fie!
for shame! What a host, so zealous! And he was

there in the hall, flat on a sheet of blood that
ran down the stairs. I did appreciate it. There are few
hosts who so thoroughly prepare to greet a guest
only casually invited, and that several months ago.

FRANK O'HARA

BREAK

Washing glasses in the sink
and the first thing she knew was this
dull click, like a tongue,
under the soap-suds.
The foam pinked.
Now she could see blood
smoking from the flap of skin,
and it was over, clearly,
out in the open:
holding water, feeling nothing.

ROBIN ROBERTSON

TWO SMALL POEMS OF DESIRE

1

The little sounds I make against your skin
don't mean anything. They make me
an animal learning vowels; not that I know
I do this, but I hear them
floating away over your shoulders, sticking
to the ceiling. *Aa Ee Iy Oh Uu.*

Are they sounds of surprise
at the strange ghosts your nakedness makes
moving above me in how much light
a net can catch?

Who cares. Sometimes language virtuously used
is language badly used. It's tough
and difficult and true to say
I love you when you do these things to me.

2

The way I prefer to play you back
is naked in the cool lawn of those green sheets,
just afterwards,
and saying *What secret am I?*

I am brought up sharp in a busy street,
staring inwards as you put down your drink
and touch me again. *How does it feel?*

It feels like tiny gardens
growing in the palms of the hands,
invisible,
sweet, if they had a scent.

CAROL ANN DUFFY

from SIX HOUSEHOLD APPLIANCES

1   HOOVER

It picks up mainly pieces of us,
Small flakes of skin, odd hairs, an eyelash,
Then paperclips and grains of food
Gone hard where they fell three weeks past.

Every so often it's fit to burst
And there's this touching scene: the bag,
Split sometimes down the middle, is lifted
From the plastic vacuum chamber
And you can see it all conjoined
In wadded bliss at last: us there
With everything we sidelined, edged
Off tables, worktops, chairs and shelves
While forging our lives on ahead.

Dumped in the bin. The bag replaced.
And I'm off roaming around the flat
Again with this huge hungry wheeze,
This loud dog on a leash, resolved
To clean up, get our lives in order.

JUSTIN QUINN

Timer

Gold survives the fire that's hot enough
to make you ashes in a standard urn.
An envelope of coarse official buff
contains your wedding ring which wouldn't burn.

Dad told me I'd to tell them at St James's
that the ring should go in the incinerator.
That 'eternity' inscribed with both their names is
his surety that they'd be together, 'later'.

I signed for the parcelled clothing as the son,
the cardy, apron, pants, bra, dress –

the clerk phoned down: *6–8–8–3–1?*
Has she still her ring on? (Slight pause) *Yes!*

It's on my warm palm now, your burnished ring!

I feel your ashes, head, arms, breasts, womb, legs,
sift through its circle slowly, like that thing
you used to let me watch to time the eggs.

Tony Harrison

NÁR MHÉANAR É

Mise 'mo shuí taobh thiar díot,
mo dhá láimh anall ort go dlúth,
an gluais-rothar ag imeacht ar luas,
abair céad míle san uair,
trí Pháirc an Fhíonuisce,
níos mire ná na fianna,
níos suaimhní ná an buar,
le breacadh lae nó um nóin,
gan duine ar bith eile ann
ar fud na páirce móire,
an bheirt againn geal-nocht,
's an rothar ag gluaiseacht go mear
fé ghrian na gcrann os ár gcionn,
gan fothram dá laghad ón inneall –
ach fuaim bheag anála na beirte.

PEARSE HUTCHINSON

Wouldn't It Be Lovely

Me on the pillion behind you,
my two arms tight around you,
the motorbike going fast
a hundred miles an hour, say,
right through the Phoenix Park,
swifter than deer,
more canty than kine,
at break-of-day or at noon,
with nobody else there
in the whole vast park,
the pair of us bright-naked,
and the bike moving fast
under the light of the sun
in the trees over our heads,
no noise at all from the engine
only the small sound
of you and me breathing.

Pearse Hutchinson

The Witches of Móinín na gCloigeann

We wax our jackets
With cooking fats
And polish our boots
With Bovril.
A trio of crabby bitches,
Or lesbian New Age witches.
The average council house coven.

We were vrooming round County Clare
In a did-it-ourselves camper van
(A 1960s ambulance from Halifax
Painted bubble-gum pink
With purple lightning flashes)
And came upon a village set into the rock.
Signposted as 'Boston'.
Subtitled 'Móinín na gCloigeann'.
Seems that some Massachusetts Man
Got the tourist equation arseways
And named the place in his likeness,
Instead of taking a piece of Ireland with him.
Personally, we prefer the real name
Of a bleached meadow bobbled with skulls.
In gesture, a cow's cranium
Hangs from our lintel, bizzie-lizzies
Bursting from the sockets.

The Rural Resettlement sorted us out
With a house (after some minor resistance
To the co-habitation of three women
In their various forties). We scrabble a living

From natural health remedying
And home-brewed aphrodisia:
Pulverised currants of goaty dung
And the morning dandelion sap that hangs
Like spit freshly mustered and spat.

And we stay in the house quite a bit,
Spinning out our afternoons
To Marty Whelan's nasal buzz
And our vicious menopausal crafting:
Schemes for the hexing
Of Lisdoon-bound mismatched men.
Unsexing their dreams of a folt
Of yellow hair and strong-beamed
Women with fields to their name.
We play poker, eat rose-hips and grow
Haggedy in this place of rocks and bones.

We wax our jackets
With cooking fats
And polish our boots
With Bovril.
A trio of crabby bitches,
Or lesbian New Age witches.
The average council house coven.

MARY O'DONOGHUE

LIPSTICK

Home from work one evening, the summer
Before I went to Iran,
I switched the radio on as usual,
Chose a knife and started to slice
Red peppers, spring onions, wild mushrooms.

It was a while before I started listening.
Propped up against a tin of Lapsang tea,
The radio on the far shelf
Was narrating a documentary about Iran.

After the Shah fled, Revolutionary Guards
Patrolled the streets of Teheran.
They were looking for stray hairs, exposed ankles
And other signs of female disrespect.
When they discovered women wearing lipstick
They razor-bladed it off,
Replacing one red gash with another.

The programme ended.
I was left standing there in my kitchen
With the vegetables half-chopped on the table:
The scarlet circles of the peppers
Delicate mouths, scattered at random.

ROSITA BOLAND

THE BRIDGE

twenty one years old evening in
the boston city public library reading
mexican history native american poetry
what ginsberg said to cassady in denver city
in nineteen forty seven and then when they kicked me out
i went to the bookshop across the street
to look at maps read a biography of dylan free

days i painted a clapboard house in cambridge
first i had to get the old flaky paint off
which took a while then i began to paint
it was a quiet street trees few people
it was peaceful working there alone
and the money wasnt bad

then covered in dust and paint
walking home in workclothes
past harvard university through old streets
of cambridge with redbrick footpaths
dreaming new york city mexico city
and all the cities that awaited me and
strange friends i hadnt met and women
on balconies in hot countries speaking
strange languages i didnt understand

one time
i remember this like yesterday
the angle of the sun
it was evening
i reached the bridge across the charles
and the bridge was leaping

across the back bays wide open maw
a sudden breeze kicked up
wild horses broke loose on open seas of grass
suddenly i was running
i was running across the sky across the water

PHILIP O'CEALLAIGH

WIDGEON

for Paul Muldoon

It had been badly shot.
While he was plucking it
he found, he says, the voice box –

like a flute stop
in the broken windpipe –

and blew upon it
unexpectedly
his own small widgeon cries.

SEAMUS HEANEY

EPILOGUE

The journey back was a nightmare.
Alice was menstrual, resentful,
complaining she always has to drive;
she was gripping the wheel at arm's length
as though appalled, repelled,
as we ripped through a sprawled
and sleeping landscape into the sky.
She seemed to be lost in a half-trance
of remembering, when the car tensed –

and the white rabbit in Alice's eye
was a stark black stare in the fast lane,
pulped by a tyre on the passenger side,
sending a shudder up through the bodywork.
I screamed, and Alice's knuckles gleamed
on the steering wheel, bright with shock,
till finally we stopped so I could be sick
on the motorway roadside grass. It was too late,
Alice whispered, We were going too fast.

COLETTE BRYCE

NOR

'There didn't have to be 2,000 diseases
of the skin,' I remember someone commenting.
Nor 17,293 painfully slow routes through the vomitory
before being thrown to the lions of death.
Nor 11,416 ways of feeling wounded.
Nor 89,010 gradations of loneliness
calibrated on traffic islands, country lanes.
Nor 29,109,352 reasons to toss and turn at night.
Nor stage fright, nor honeymoon cystitis.
Nor *esprit de l'escalier*, nor so many calories in cream.
Nor sexually transmitted fatalities, nor smoker's cough.
Nor 250,000,000 tons (live weight) of humanity
to experience these things, nor however many
newborn pounds were dragged screaming, added
to the tally, since my opening line.

DENNIS O'DRISCOLL

10 x 10 x 10

One winter evening, Donald travelled the
15 miles to his girlfriend's home town and,
disliking her parents, decided to
phone her house and arrange to rendezvous
at the end of her road rather than call
for her and have to face her mum and dad.
Her mother answered the phone and said that
Susan was visiting a friend nextdoor.
'Where are you ringing from?' 'Oh, I'm at home.'
(He was, in fact, only round the corner.)

Having put down the phone, he decided
to walk to the house nextdoor to Susan's,
collect her from there and go to the pub
(thus still avoiding her parents). He set
off along the road where the kiosk was
and, after a few minutes, turned at right
angles into Susan's road and sauntered
towards her friend's; when all of a sudden
out of the pitch darkness bounded a dog
which he recognised as Sue's Dalmatian.

A distant street-light illumined a pair,
identified by Don as Sue's parents
(which identification was confirmed
by her mother's voice shouting 'Heel, Measles!' –
he well knew both voice and nomenclature).
Rightly judging that they might find it odd
to encounter one who had telephoned
only five minutes ago and told them
emphatically that he was 15 miles
distant, he panicked and turned on his heel.

He walked briskly away from them, but thought,
as he passed under a sodium light,
that they might recognise him, so he hunched
his back – hoping thus to disguise his frame.
He lacked confidence in this, however,
and to consolidate his disguise he
affected a limp – first left leg, then right.
Thus, alternating legs, he limped faster
and faster away from her parents, till
he was limp-sprinting at 10 m.p.h.

But Measles, who knew him, tore after him,
yelping and biting his trouser leg. 'Down,
bad Measles!' he whispered between clenched teeth
while oscillating extravagantly.
He paused at the corner, smacked Measles' snout,
said 'Damn and blast it all to bloody Hell!',
ran his fastest (unhampered by Measles
and now using conventional techniques)
and thought 'This could be good to write about –
but in the third person, naturally.'

On another occasion, Donald was
out drinking with a friend when closing time
came, so, wishing to continue their chat,
they went to a theatre which also
had a restaurant serving drinks till 12.
Drinks were only served to people dining
and, not wanting anything to eat, Don
went to the bar for two pints of bitter.
'No drinks without meals, sir.' 'Oh, we've just got
our meal, over on that table.' he lied.

'You're a bloody liar – you've only just
come in. Get out. You're not getting served.' So
he left by one of three doors and went down
a dark corridor. But it must have been
the wrong door, because he found himself in
a huge auditorium – house lights dimmed,
only the stage lights ablaze – completely
deserted. He stumbled along the aisle
to the stage, which he mounted, noticing
a stage *on* the stage – 10 x 10 x 10.

He clambered up to the stage on the stage
and sang Maurice Chevalier numbers,
danced to the empty auditorium.
'Evry leel briz sim to weesper Looiz.
Eef a natingel coo sing lak you. Sank
Even for leetel girls – zey grow up in
ze mos delightfool away. Ooh la la!
Eet is – ow you Eenglish say? – saucy, no?'
Behind him, twenty feet high, he noticed
a catwalk reached by a metal ladder.

He climbed the ladder and danced along the
foot-wide catwalk. 'Evry leel briz sim to' –
suddenly he lost balance and fell but
clutched at the back-drapes to save himself and
thought 'I am an interloper, therefore
I must do nothing to damage this hall.'
Thinking his weight would rip the curtains, he
let go, fell down a few feet, grabbed hold, then
let go again and grabbed hold again till
the fabric began to tear and conscience

forced Don to let go for fear of damage.
*   *   *   *   *   *   *   *   *   *
*   *   *   *   *   *   *   *   *   *
*   *   *   *   *   *   When he regained
consciousness, he was considering the
arbitrary nature of the Sonnet –
'One might as well invent any kind of
structure (ten stanzas each of ten lines each
of ten syllables might be a good one),
the subject-matter could be anything.'

PETER READING

To No One

Her husband passed on the street outside.
She watched, said softly to no one:
'The things you'd see passin' the window
When you wouldn't have a gun.'

Brendan Kennelly

Nagging Misunderstanding

Let me clear up a nagging misunderstanding: This
is the way to make the white woman's bed; she thinks
I make it because she is rich, she thinks I make it
to get her money, that I can't get money any other
way, no skills, no intelligence, no contribution to
society but for her four poster, but I make her bed
because on Judgement Day, you will have to sleep
in the bed you made and I make damn good ones but
she didn't make any.

Thylias Moss

A GLIMPSE OF THE GODDESS

for Noel Monaghan

God, I wish I was a young Guard's wife in Granard
in the 60s, full of promise and hopping with hormones
long before it was fully known what a hormone was, but
these young women knew their power
and how well a young Guard looked
in uniform. A fine thing just come in from the hayfields
of Ballygar and places like it, to sit and swing upon a chair
in the barracks, refreshingly cool on balmy days.

A place with wainscoting, regulation stationery
and a surly sergeant, not a bad auld bollix really,
behind it all, loves the auld flowers, has the place
crawling with them and hanging baskets,
if you're not vexed.
The young Guards pedal slowly out into the damp places
to gather moss for him, soft and interwoven moss,
where he might lay his salvias and brightly coloured
petunias.

The young Guards sit and swing in the cool, within,
dreaming of noxious weeds and the odd marauding dog.
That's right.
And preserving the scene.
Wondering if hair on the upper lip should be encouraged,
it might seem a biteen silly when hurling with the local
team, the lads might slag the hell out of him –
but still a moustache looks well on Mahony up in
Kilinaleck.

The young Guard's wife is not cramped in or held
high in a tower of stone, no, she glides along a hallway
to a mahogany door, with a fluff of soft pink stuff at her
      feet
and a half-concealed negligée of pink chiffon quite full
under the flowing dressing-gown . . .
Himself is doing nights and dreams now in the warmth
of their bed of ragwort and fields full of milky thistles,
and go-boys loitering with intent . . .
But she comes to the mahogany door tasting of toast and
marmalade.

There is hope and heaven in the very smooth skin
which plunges down from the curve of her neck,
down into places of slight damp and scented nooks.
– It's your milk, ma'am, two bottles.
The young poet stands there with his father's milk in his
hand.
He is in a paroxysm of creative passion which will burst
and rip all innocence right out of him.

The image of the inspiring goddess will stay with him
for the rest of his life,
if now he could only disentangle his knees, his balls,
and the two empty milk bottles
the young Guard's wife passes
to him slowly across
the threshold.

RITA KELLY

Seven Things Wasted on Lovers

1
Diving boards. Lovers
prefer to lounge.

2
Restaurant seats.
Have you ever actually seen them
actually eat?

3
Pyjamas (this includes bed socks).

4
Gardens: of Eden,
chosen, secret or hanging gardens;
garden gnomes.

5
Sunrises, sunsets, sunspots,
eclipses of the moon.

6
Mythology, history, politics, psychology, chess.

7
Oh, and apples,
obviously, Eve.
(How many is that?)

Pat Boran

Saturday Afternoon in Dublin

Dietrich Fischer-Dieskau is in the process
of depressing me singing
the 'Der Einsame in Herbst' section
of *Das Lied von der Erde*.
A flute is playing as I look
at my sisters photographed in New York
in a crowd of twenty-five thousand people
getting ready for a bicycle tour.
I meet them for a few days
every two years or so
but I don't know them any more;
only how they used to be
before I went away.
Are you crying yet?
Sometimes you get to know your relatives
better when they're pinned down
like butterfly specimens
wearing baseball cap and crash helmet respectively.
Kate, I see, has a blue-faced watch
with snappy red band.
Ellen has let her hair grow.
They both smile nervously
because my father is taking the picture
in the middle of the throng.
Dietrich, meanwhile, has moved on to a beautiful, sad
song with harps – I'm glad I don't know any German –
it's even sadder hearing words sung
that make no sense.
He says 'Ja, ja' better than anyone.
It isn't music for New York, really.
A Hopper etching: *Night Shadows,*

an afternoon in Dublin looking
out the arid window for inspiration,
wanting so many things to happen –
that's when it get to you.
Are you crying yet?

Julie O'Callaghan

The Wall I Built

The wall I built
the sea took.

The stones I gathered
the sea scattered.

Falling asleep I look
left, right,

because, you see,
they don't make

tomorrow like
they used to.

Dermot Healy

ADVICE TO A POET

Be a chauffeur, my father said
And never mind the poetry.
That's all very well for the rich
They can afford it.
What you need is money in your belt
Free uniform and plenty of travel.
Besides that, there's nothing in verse.
And all poets are raging homosexuals.

I'd still like to be a poet.

Another thing: don't ever marry
And if you do, then marry for cash.
Love, after all, is easily come by
And any old whore will dance for a pound.
Take my advice and be a chauffeur
The uniform will suit you a treat
Marriage and poems will blind you surely
And poets and lovers are doomed to hell.

I'd still like to be a poet.

But where's the sense in writing poetry?
Did any poet ever make good?
I never met one who wasn't a pauper
A prey to bailiffs, lawyers and priests.
Take my advice and be a chauffeur
With your appearance you're bound to do well
You might even meet some rich old widow
Who'll leave you a fortune the moment she dies.

I'd still like to be a poet.

Well, blast you then, your days are darkened
Poverty, misery, carnage and sin.
The poems you write won't be worth a penny.
And the women you marry will bleed you to death.
Take my advice and buy a revolver
Shoot yourself now in the back of the head.
The Government then might raise a subscription
To keep your poor father from breeding again.

PATRICK GALVIN

THE INSTRUMENT

I woke to someone vacuuming in a nearby corridor,
that merciless mechanical whine getting nearer and noisier,
battering the skirting-boards at every turn,
sucking up the dust to which we shall return.

On our deathday it won't be whippoorwills
clouding the window, chorusing for our souls,
nor banshees nor spectres from a neglected tomb,
but down the corridor, in a not too distant room

someone will switch on a vacuum.

MARK GRANIER

THE WORDSWORTH GOES ON A JOURNEY

Once there was a Wordsworth,
And this Wordsworth
Was very wise
And very, very frugal,

And the wise, frugal Wordsworth went visiting
Many different places, up and down
The big, big island where he lived.
See the big, big island?

And because the Wordsworth was so wise and so frugal –
Mark, can you tell us what 'frugal' is?
That's right, it means the Wordsworth
Never, never lost things.
He saved them
And kept them with him.

Well, because the Wordsworth was so wise
And so frugal,
Every one of the journeys he made
Helped the Wordsworth in his trade,
Which was the making of verses.
Every trip he took, up and down
The big island, gave him verses,
Which gave him silver coins, which gave him
A house on a very nice,
Very pretty lake.
See the lake?
Isn't it nice?
Bobby, can you see the lake in the back?

But . . .
What do you think happened then?
Well . . . the Wordsworth took a trip
Which gave him
Nothing at all!
Not a line, not a shilling!
A shilling is a kind of money.
But he had none!
He came home with his pockets empty!
See the empty pockets?
Laura, can you see the empty pockets?
See how unhappy the Wordsworth looks?

Now:
Where do you think he went,
The Wordsworth,
On this special journey?

Well . . .
This one, special trip
The Wordsworth took
Was to 'Ireland'. 'Ireland'
Was a not-quite-so-big
Island next to the big island
Where the Wordsworth lived.
See?
Yes, it looks like a kitty.
And what does the big, big island look like?

Bobby, be quiet.

JOHN DOLAN

MARGINALIA

Sometimes the notes are ferocious,
skirmishes against the author
raging along the borders of every page
in tiny black script.
If I could just get my hands on you,
Kierkegaard, or Conor Cruise O'Brien,
they seem to say,
I would bolt the door and beat some logic into your head.

Other comments are more offhand, dismissive –
'Nonsense.' 'Please!' 'HA!!' –
that kind of thing.
I remember once looking up from my reading,
my thumb as a bookmark,
trying to imagine what the person must look like
who wrote, 'Don't be a ninny'
alongside a paragraph in *The Life of Emily Dickinson*.

Students are more modest
needing to leave only their splayed footprints
along the shore of the page.
One scrawls 'Metaphor' next to a stanza of Eliot's.
Another notes the presence of 'Irony'
fifty times outside the paragraphs of *A Modest Proposal*.

Or they are fans who cheer from the empty bleachers,
hands cupped around their mouths.
'Absolutely,' they shout
to Duns Scotus and James Baldwin.
'Yes.' 'Bull's-eye.' 'My man!'
Check marks, asterisks, and exclamation points
rain down along the sidelines.

And if you have managed to graduate from college
without ever having written 'Man vs. Nature'
in a margin, perhaps now
is the time to take one step forward.

We have all seized the white perimeter as our own
and reached for a pen if only to show
we did not just laze in an armchair turning pages;
we pressed a thought into the wayside,
planted an impression along the verge.

Even Irish monks in their cold scriptoria
jotted along the borders of the Gospels
brief asides about the pain of copying,
a bird singing near their window,
or the sunlight that illuminated their page –
anonymous men catching a ride into the future
on a vessel more lasting than themselves.

And you have not read Joshua Reynolds,
they say, until you have read him
enwreathed with Blake's furious scribbling.

Yet the one I think of most often,
the one that dangles from me like a locket,
was written in the copy of *Catcher in the Rye*
I borrowed from the local library
one slow, hot summer.
I was just beginning high school then,
reading books on a davenport in my parents' living room,
and I cannot tell you
how vastly my loneliness was deepened,
how poignant and amplified the world before me seemed,
when I found on one page

a few greasy looking smears
and next to them, written in soft pencil –
by a beautiful girl, I could tell,
whom I would never meet –
'Pardon the egg salad stains, but I'm in love.'

BILLY COLLINS

THE UNCERTAINTY OF THE POET

'The Tate Gallery yesterday announced that it had paid £1 million for a Giorgio de Chirico masterpiece, The Uncertainty of the Poet. *It depicts a torso and a bunch of bananas.'*
                                                    Guardian, 2 April 1985

I am a poet.
I am very fond of bananas.

I am bananas.
I am very fond of a poet.

I am a poet of bananas.
I am very fond.

A fond poet of 'I am, I am' –
Very bananas.

Fond of 'Am I bananas?
Am I?' – a very poet.

Bananas of a poet!
Am I fond? Am I very?

Poet bananas! I am.
I am fond of a 'very'.

I am of very fond bananas.
Am I a poet?

WENDY COPE

BURYING THE ELEPHANT

What a grave it took to dig,
burying the elephant,
his shadow lengthened and grew dark,
his shadow rolled over and was gone.
O shock of the spirit when
great things go down.

He was caught in the sun's net,
the sun brought him crashing down,
elephant spirit meeting the ground;
blue eyes muddied with a failure to rise,
earth's yawn must bury him now.

The elephant was heavy-blooded,
stone full, slow with time;
we all came to bury him,
our blue eyes lit with ivory
and a kind of grief;

I had my own pit dug,
feet up, my animal kicked
with stiff limbs; in my hide
my shadow rolled on the grass and groaned,
my spirit grew dark and gave;
elephant trumpet bellowed in the trees,
the forest sank to its knees,
the forest rose and swayed.

What a grave it took
to bury my animal's meat.
I turned his spirit out and now
the darkness is complete.

SARA BERKELEY

THE GREAT BLASKET ISLAND

Six men born on this island
have come back after twenty-one years.
They climb up the overgrown roads
to their family houses
and come out shaking their heads.
The roofs have fallen in
and birds have nested in the rafters.
All the white-washed rooms
all the nagging and praying
and scolding and giggling
and crying and gossiping
are scattered in the memories of these men.
One says, 'Ten of us, blown to the winds –
some in England, some in America, some in Dublin.
Our whole way of life – extinct.'
He blinks back the tears
and looks across the island
past the ruined houses, the cliffs
and out to the horizon.

Listen, mister, most of us cry sooner or later
over a Great Blasket Island of our own.

JULIE O'CALLAGHAN

DONNELLY'S BUS

On Donnelly's Bus
All the dead passengers sit up.
I hear skeleton conversations
Rattling down the aisle,
Archie, the ghost driver
Overfeeding the throttle.

On Donnelly's Bus
Phantom passengers lean on gravestones.
The man with the pipe is an Indian Chief
Lost to a language of smoke.
Gent Geraghty's white scarf is wrapped
Tight as a bandage round his throat.

On Donnelly's Bus
Dream faces peer
Through beads of rain
At waltzing fields and ditches.
Elmbank Chickens in cardboard boxes
Peck at the light in my head.

NOEL MONAGHAN

IN THE COUNTRY

In the country there are youths
With the sweet breath of sucky calves
And their soft mouths.

ANNE HAVERTY

KEEPING THINGS WHOLE

In a field
I am the absence
of field.
This is
always the case.
Wherever I am
I am what is missing.

When I walk
I part the air
and always
the air moves in
to fill the spaces
where my body's been.

We all have reasons
for moving.
I move
to keep things whole.

MARK STRAND

Six

The blond medallions of the aspen
shook and burned on the first day

of summer. I wore my gingham pinny
and no knickers and waved wildly

at the boats rounding the bay,
snagging the waters to a silver V.

Granny had her wound dressed
as usual in her cool dark room.

Mummy made scrambled eggs for tea.
Charlie and I jumped like fleas

off the old stone house and fell
giggling to the grassy bank.

One, two, three steps back
for a good long run, four, five, six . . .

I stepped into nothing.
Fragments of green and brown glass

tore the gingham pinafore
as I came to and Charlie stared

frog-eyed at my arm, bent
improbably back at the elbow.

In hospital, Kermit looked peeved

about the confiscated chocolates
and sulked at the end of my bed.
Granny saw gingham in her dreams,

vanishing over a cliff-edge.
Every day the student doctors came

and took more notes, staring
and rattling their stethoscopes.

I fretted in the wicker chair,
inserting a knitting-needle

inside the dusty cast, always
missing the itch by inches.

I couldn't tell what I'd broken.
Charlie was suddenly childish,

and anyway, he was a boy.
I collected autographs and pouted.

When they finally sawed the cast off,
my arm, like a helium balloon, floated.

CAITRÍONA O'REILLY

EIRATA

after Paul Muldoon

for 'Armagh' read 'Armani'
for 'brat' read 'Brut'
for 'Carmelite' read 'Camel light'
for 'Dáil' read 'doll'
for 'exiles' read 'X-files'
for 'faction' read 'fiction'
for 'Georgian' read 'Georgics'
for 'hallowed' read 'hollowed'
for 'island' read 'inland'
for 'jarvey' read 'Charvet'
for 'Kerry' read 'curry'
for 'Ludo' read 'Lotto'
for 'Mallow' read 'mellow'
for 'novena' read 'novella'
for 'Ógra' read 'Oprah'
for 'parish' read 'perish'
for 'Quoof' read 'Quiff'
for 'rosary' read 'Rotary'
for 'sacred' read 'scared'
for 'traitor' read 'trattoria'
for 'Ulster' read 'Hustler'
for 'virtuous' read 'virtual'
for 'widows' read 'Windows'
for 'X-rated' read 'X-rayed'
for 'yawp' read 'yob'
for 'zed' read 'zee'

IGGY MCGOVERN

In the Holiday Inn

After the party I returned to the hotel.
The room was too hot so I took off my coat.

It was January but I turned down the thermostat.
I took off my shirt but I was still too hot.

I opened the window, it was snowing outside.
Despite all this the air began to simmer.

The room had a pyrexia of unknown origin.
I took off my trousers, I took off my shorts.

This room was a cauldron, this room was tropical.
On the wall, the picture of willows changed

to palm trees. In the mirror I could see the desert.
I stood naked in my socks and juggled

with pomegranates. I offered offerings
that soon became burnt. This was some holiday.

I took off one sock and read the bible.
They were cremating idols, sacrificing oxen.

I could feel the heat of their fiery furnace.
I could hear those pyromaniacs chanting.

I could smell the singed wings of cherubim.
I took off the other sock and began to dance.

Like sand the carpet scalded my twinkling feet.
Steam was coming out of both my ears.

I was King David dancing before the Lord.
Outside it was snowing but inside it was Israel.

I danced six cubits this way, six cubits that.
Now at dawn I'm hotter than the spices of Sheba.

What shall I do? I shall ask my wise son,
Solomon. Where are you Solomon?

You are not yet born, you do not know
how wise you are or that I'm your father

and that I'm dancing and dancing.

DANNIE ABSE

THEY EAT OUT

In restaurants we argue
over which of us will pay for your funeral

though the real question is
whether or not I will make you immortal.

At the moment only I
can do it and so

I raise the magic fork
over the plate of beef fried rice

and plunge it into your heart.
There is a faint pop, a sizzle

and through your own split head
you rise up glowing:

the ceiling opens
a voice sings Love Is A Many

Splendoured Thing
you hang suspended above the city

in blue tights and a red cape,
your eyes flashing in unison.

The other diners regard you
some with awe, some only with boredom:

they cannot decide if you are a new weapon
or only a new advertisement.

As for me, I continue eating;
I liked you better the way you were,
but you were always ambitious.

MARGARET ATWOOD

IT IS AN OFFENCE

The man in the flats opposite keeps a whippet
(once a racer) and two or three times a week
it craps by my front door – sloped, weary turds
like a single file of slugs in battle fatigues
(surprisingly slow for a whippet) – so that often
my shoes, my wife's, our children's bring it back home
to the stairs, the skirting, the carpets, the kitchen tiles
in bobbles or flakes or hanks or outrageous slithery smears.

The sad old dog doesn't know what he's doing, and yet
I'd still like to cover his arsehole with quick-set cement.

I admit that I also yearn to leave my mark on society,
and not see machines or people trample it foolishly.

On the one hand it's only shit; on the other, shit's shit,
and what we desire in the world is less, not more, of it.

ANDREW MOTION

THE BACK OF MY HAND

I know myself like the back of my hand.
I rarely glance at the back of my hand.
Question me not about the back of my hand.

BRENDAN KENNELLY

ROLES

Emily Brontë's cleaning the car:
water sloshes over her old trainers
as she scrubs frail blood-shapes from the windscreen
and swirls the hose-jet across the roof.
When it's done she'll go to the supermarket;
then, if she has to, face her desk.

I'm striding on the moor in my hard shoes,
a shawl over my worsted bodice,
the hem of my skirt scooping dew from the grass
as I pant up towards the breathless heights.
I'll sit on a rock I know and write a poem.
It may not come out as I intend.

FLEUR ADCOCK

The Visionary

The woman in the sweet shop
is turning into her mother.
Only the other week
she was young
when talk of weddings,
wallpaper, new fridges
and a small flat in the town was all talk.

Then for God knows why
he took a bus that never stopped
and she was left
with the wallpaper shame
of not having any fruit in her womb
that she might buy
white socks for.

Her mother's tiredness
grew into her,
her mannerisms,
her thanks be to Gods.

When she totted up the numbers
she wore her mother's glasses.
She joked about it,

'Sure what difference does it make
haven't me and mammy
the same vision anyway,
aren't we both far sighted?'

Rita Ann Higgins

COURTSHIP

There is a girl you like so you tell her
your penis is big, but that you cannot get yourself
to use it. Its demands are ridiculous, you say,
even self-defeating, but to be honoured somehow,
briefly, inconspicuously in the dark.

When she closes her eyes in horror,
you take it all back. You tell her you're almost
a girl yourself and can understand why she is shocked.
When she is about to walk away, you tell her
you have no penis, that you don't

know what got into you. You get on your knees.
She suddenly bends down to kiss your shoulder and you know
you're on the right track. You tell her you want
to bear children and that is why you seem confused.
You wrinkle your brow and curse the day you were born.

She tries to calm you, but you lose control.
You reach for her panties and beg forgiveness as you do.
She squirms and you howl like a wolf. Your craving
seems monumental. You know you will have her.
Taken by storm, she is the girl you will marry.

MARK STRAND

7Up, Torremolinos

The icy fizz numbs my tongue.
Curving far out, a star-bright
arc-weld of beach on a calm
black sea. The universe is utterly
beyond me, but close. Close.

Mark Granier

Pep-Talk to Poets from Their Sales Manager

for Gerald Dawe

Alright, you Irish guys –
first off – I love ya – got it?
Hey – where's the blarney?
Quit looking like you were just included
in a 'Contemporary British Poetry' anthology
or something; we got books to sell!
Now, what abouta few Volkswagens in bogs
or grey streets with graffiti on the walls –
scenes like that;
you haven't been turning it out lately.
How come? I need stuff with slogans, guys.
Folksy stuff – know what I mean?
I'm doing my best but it's all lookin
a little like a yawner at this stage.
That's all, lads – keep at it.

I wanna see all a you extra-terrestrials
gravitating over here double quick, fellas.
'Take me to yer reader' – right, guys?
Now let's get serious – huh?
Here's your sales chart – up, up, up!
Kinda like a flying saucer discovering
new universes of humanoids who wanna book of poetry.
We're gonna capture new markets, aren't we,
and no more traitors writing
transvestite translations or we'll zap them
with our lazer gun – right?

Goils! Move yer feminist little butts over here.
Yer doins terrific. Lots of sarcasm
about what termites we guys are, lots of PMT,
lots of mothers acting square – magnificent!
My god, you're going great guns, ladies.
OOPS! I mean WOMEN don't I?
We want a lot of hype comin up to Christmas
so those cash registers keep singing.
Just one word of advice: see if you can
Virginia Woolf-up your images a bit
and who knows what we can do?
Sisterhood is powerful!

All miscellaneous misfits, up front please.
Lookit pals, *you* want an easy life,
I wanta easy life and *we all* want super-sales,
so why not give up this poetic individuality baloney
and get yourselves an angle, join a group.
My job is tough enough
without you weirdos
lousing it up even more!

Julie O'Callaghan

Seven Unpopular Things to Say About Blood

1
Our mothers bled, and bleed,
and our enemies,
and our enemies' mothers.

2
It rushes to the finest
nick, romances the blade.

3
It dreams
the primary dream of liquids:
to sleep, horizontally.

4
It is in the surgeon's heart,
the executioner's brain.

5
Vampires and journalists
are excited by it; poets
faint on sight.

6
I knew it better as a child,
kept scabs, like ladybugs, in jars.

7
Blood: now mine would be with yours
until the moon breaks orbit
and the nights run cold.

Pat Boran

THE ACT

My brother knows how to jive.
I saw him dancing in the back yard.
A shifting grace across the bare ground.
His suit jacket flapping.
When men dance like that
They want to be their fathers,
To stop all other movement.
It is an act of delirium.

JOSEPH HORGAN

WIDENING THE CANAL

The oldest sister is ground-breaker
For all the girls who follow after.
Her birth takes that bit longer:
She widens the canal. Makes it stronger.

The youngest sister slips through quickest.
The canal at its broadest, she is the littlest.
Plenty of room to wriggle and slither,
Jerking her safety rope along the route with her.

MARY O'DONOGHUE

Sometime During Eternity . . .

Sometime during eternity
                    some guys show up
and one of them
            who shows up real late
                        is a kind of carpenter
        from some square-type place
                    like Galilee
        and he starts wailing
                    and claiming he is hip
        to who made heaven
                    and earth
                            and that the cat
            who really laid it on us
                        is his Dad

And moreover
    he adds
            It's all writ down
                    on some scroll-type parchments
        which some henchmen
            leave lying around the Dead Sea somewheres
        a long time ago
                    and which you won't even find
    for a coupla thousand years or so
                    or at least for
    nineteen hundred and fortyseven
                        of them
            to be exact
                    and even then
        nobody really believes them
                        or me
                            for that matter

You're hot
                they tell him
And they cool him

They stretch him on the Tree to cool

            And everybody after that
                                is always making models
                    of this Tree
                            with Him hung up
    and always crooning His name
                    and calling Him to come down
                    and sit in
                            on their combo
            as if he is *the* king cat
                                who's got to blow
        or they can't quite make it

        Only he don't come down
                                from His Tree

Him just hang there
                on His Tree
looking real Petered out
                and real cool
                            and also
        according to a roundup
                            of late world news
        from the usual unreliable sources
                                real dead

LAWRENCE FERLINGHETTI

Sad Sun

Oh sun. Oh sun,
Oh sun. How does
it feel to be
blocked by the
dark, dark clouds?

Oh child
it doesn't really
feel bad at all
not at all not at
all not at all

Nicholas Sanz-Gould

Treacle

Funny to think you can still buy it now,
a throwback, like shoe polish or the sardine key.
When you lever the lid it opens with a sigh
and you're face-to-face with history.
By that I mean the unstable pitch black
you're careful not to spill, like mercury

that doesn't give any reflection back,
that gets between the cracks of everything
and holds together the sandstone and bricks
of our museums and art galleries;
and though those selfsame buildings stand
hosed clean now of all their gunk and soot,

feel the weight of this tin in your hand,
read its endorsement from one Abram Lyle
'Out of the strong came forth sweetness'
below the weird logo of bees in swarm
like a halo over the lion carcass.
Breathe its scent, something lost from our streets

like horseshit or coalsmoke; its base note
a building block as biblical as honey,
the last dregs of an empire's dark sump;
see how a spoonful won't let go of its past,
what the tin calls back to the mean of its lip
as you pour its contents over yourself

and smear it into every orifice.
You're history now, a captive explorer
staked out for the insects; you're tarred
and feel its caul harden. The restorer
will tap your details back out of the dark:
close-in work with a toffee hammer.

PAUL FARLEY

WORLD EXPO, BRISBANE

After a hot day spent queuing
to see exhibitions from many countries
On the theme of 'Leisure and Technology',
I came upon the Pacific Islands pavilion
And stayed a long time
Watching two nautilus shells
Glimmering, pearl-coloured,
Swaying and yielding in the water
Very delicately making love.

ROSITA BOLAND

AT THE JUNCTION

There is the hum of car-windows closing.
Even the sunroofs slip shut with a sigh
As refugees at the red light infiltrate
The lane discipline of our stalled drive-time.

Some brat of an Indo-European lavishes
Lather on my own clean windscreen.
The wipers stop, stuck in the slush,
Like the wartime whitewashed windowpanes

Of a tram that crossed though the Warsaw ghetto.
But I won't be blackmailed by sob stories,
I who drive an economy Opel
From outpatients to outpatients,

A middle-aged manic depressive male
Whose gifts at the altar are all
Wafer-thin, watered down, tactical;
And who hardly remembers the time or the day

When Masahiko from Tokyo came
To a Cabinteely cul-de-sac
And the children there queued up in a line
To stroke his goatee beard like a bell-rope,

Its sleek silvery Shinto softness
Shining and winding its way down
To where I could see the pawprints of infants,
A moon looming over a hangnail.

AIDAN MATHEWS

Autumn Evening

1   DOWN

They're home. It's evening. He's just sat down to winnow
Through human-interest stories in the papers.
She's staring.
                    – Here's one about Brazilian paupers . . .
She suddenly pounces on him and with no
Good reason bundles him skilfully out the window.
Oh, she'll go back to chopping the red peppers,
But first of all she gathers up the papers
And checks in passing if she's since become a widow.

Meanwhile the man has done his dozen cartwheels
Past floor after floor of their apartment block
And hit the deck beside the building's entry
In a difficult yoga position. Cools his heels.
His face has set hard in a look of shock
That his good wife was someone else entirely.

2   UP

Entirely dead, beyond all Medicare,
He nonetheless wakes up, his clothes still sodden
With blood and guts that spilled out everywhere
On settling into his new pied-à-terre.
They spill back in again. All of a sudden
He finds himself flung upwards through the air

And being grappled into the apartment
By his good wife: she struggles with all her might
Against the monstrous pull of gravity

148

For him. She wins. They hug. He reads the papers
For half an hour or so, relieved and heartened
That they've pulled through, that things will be all right,
Until she tells him that the dinner's ready –
A stew of pork, adzuki, nuts and peppers.

JUSTIN QUINN

ADDRESS SEARCH

And you will find me
any night
now, try
at the motherless sky.
com

How dare you
interrupt
me.com

I'm sorry
I was ever born.com

No doubt
you can always find
me any
time, any
where

in the damned world

FRANZ WRIGHT

On Not Winning the Kavanagh Award for the Umpteenth Time

I mailed my poems to Monaghan,
brown paper wrapped, tied up with cord,
ten pounds enclosed to help me win
The Paddy Kavanagh Award

The poems were rural, the meal bin,
the turf stack and the new-mown sward,
in form and rhyme designed to win
The Paddy Kavanagh Award

They tarried here and there with Sin
and had a note of bleak discord.
I hungered for the day I'd win
The Paddy Kavanagh Award

They showed the woman deep within:
my muse, my oracle, my Gord-
ian Knot, one snip and I would win
The Paddy Kavanagh Award

My hopes, alas, were paper-thin.
They failed to strike the proper chord
and (feck 'em!) judged unfit to win
The Paddy Kavanagh Award

For Angels dancing on a pin,
The North in peaceable accord
are safer bets than me to win
The Paddy Kavanagh Award

I should have held on to my tin
for, truth to tell, I doubt, O Lord,
if Paddy Kavanagh would win
The Paddy Kavanagh Award!

IGGY MCGOVERN

WORLD MUSIC

Okay. Elvis is driving inland
in a black Morris Minor
and white studded shirt. What else?
He's singing, of course,

a patch-up job on 'Sweet Vale of Avoca'
and 'When they begin . . . ' It's 1974.
He's seen it all. Even today
he's been through Keenagh,

Ballymahon, Tubberclair.
The names are getting longer
and he's flicking butts, like Hansel,
in a trail. He wants out.

But not before his head-to-head
with the Bethlehem Céilí Band
and their full-throttle version of,
of all things, 'Blue Suede Shoes'.

So just when he's coming up to our gate
I'm ready for him with my book and pen.
Nothing surprises Elvis. He throws me
half a smile and a cigarette stub

that I swoop on, almost dropping,
in the process, my crêpe-paper flag
with its red, stapled stripes
and its thirty-two pointless, tinfoil stars.

VONA GROARKE

GOING OUT FOR CIGARETTES

It's a story as famous as the three little pigs:
one evening a man says he is going out for cigarettes,
closes the door behind him and is never heard from again,
not one phone call, not even a postcard from Rio.

For all anyone knows, he walks straight into the distance
like a line from Euclid's notebooks and vanishes
with the smoke he blows into the soft humid air,
smoke that forms a screen, smoke to calm the bees within.

He has his fresh pack, an overcoat with big pockets.
What else does he need as he walks beyond city limits,
past the hedges, porch lights and empty cars of the suburbs
and into a realm no larger than his own hat size?

Alone, he is a solo for piano that never comes to an end,
a small plane that keeps flying away from the earth.
He is the last line of a poem that continues off the page
and down to a river to drag there in the cool flow,

questioning the still pools with its silver hook.
Let us say this is the place where the man who goes out
for cigarettes finally comes to rest: on a riverbank
above the long, inquisitive wriggling of that line,

sitting content in the quiet picnic of consciousness,
nothing on his mind as he lights up another one,
nothing but the arc of the stone bridge he notices
downstream, and its upturned reflection in the water.

BILLY COLLINS

POSTMODERN

Boy gets haud o' this porno movie, heavy Swedish number,
    broon-wrapper joab, like. Waants tae mak a copy o' it
but he's only got the ae video machine. So he thinks: Eh ken.
    Gets oot the camcorder that's been lehn gaitherin stoor
in the cupboard since last Christmas, sets it up on a wee table
    right opposite the telly, lines up the screen in the eyepiece.
Nae bather. Lets it roll. When it's feenished he checks the start
    o' the copy jist tae mak sure it's recorded okay. Nae sweat.
Dead chuffed wi' hisel. Taks it doon the pub that night and
    lends it tae his pal, then *his* pal borrys it, exetera exetera.
A fortnight later a' cunt in the pub's seen it, and some boy he
    disnae ken hands it back to him, funny smile on his puss.

Thinks nothin' o' it tho. Onywiy, three weeks later, the boy
    thinks, Ach, the wife's oot, Eh'll hae another squint
at thon video again. Same as before, oot wi' the big box o'
    Scotties, the wife's cocoa-butter, slaps in the video,
settles back in the settee, breeks down, cock oot. So he's sittin' there
    gien it big licks, a' these Swedes gien it laldy on the telly,
when he notices the reflection o' himsel, wankin awa on the screen,
    clear as day. Then he stops wankin. But his reflection disnae.
That's cuz it's no his fuckin reflection. He's only jist taped
    himsel haein a wank, huzzee. Dye no' get it? Will Eh
    hae tae *explain* it tae ye?

DON PATERSON

Courage, a Tale

There was a Child
who heard from another Child
that if you masturbate 100 times
it kills you.

This gave him pause;
he certainly slowed down quite a bit
and also
        kept count.

But, till number 80,
was relatively loose about it.
There did seem plenty of time left.

The next 18
were reserved for celebrations,
like the banquet room in a hotel.

The 99th time
was simply unavoidable.

Weeks passed.

And then he thought
Fuck it
        it's worth dying for,

and half an hour later
the score rose from 99 to 105.

Thom Gunn

The Poets

Dannie ABSE was born in Cardiff in 1923 and – like William Carlos Williams – is both poet and medical doctor. His *White Coat, Purple Coat: Collected Poems 1948–1988* was published in 1990.

Fleur ADCOCK was born in Auckland, New Zealand, in 1934 but settled in London in the early 1960s, where she worked as a librarian before deciding to write full-time. Her *Poems 1960–2000* was published in 2000.

Sherman ALEXIE is from Wellpinit, Washington, on the Spokane Indian Reservation. His first collection was *The Business of Fancydancing* (1992), a collection of stories and poems. In his poem 'On the Amtrak from Boston to New York City', he refers to the musician Don Henley, formerly of the Eagles, who organised benefit concerts to save Walden Pond, which had been threatened by developers.

ANONYMOUS: what does one say, but 'Long live anonymous'? In the case of 'The Tortoise', the poem won first prize in a schools poetry competition judged by Paul Muldoon.

Simon ARMITAGE was born in 1963 in Huddersfield and grew up in West Yorkshire. He studied Geography at Portsmouth, studied Social Science at Manchester and wrote an MA on the psychology of television violence. He has published several collections (*Zoom!, Kid, Book of Matches, The Dead Sea Poems, Cloudcuckooland*) and a *Selected Poems*. He published a prose work, *All Points North*, on life in the north of England and a novel, *Little Green Man,* in 2001.

Margaret ATWOOD was born in 1939 and has written poetry throughout her writing life as a novelist. 'It simply happened, suddenly, in 1956,' she says, 'while I was crossing the football field on the way home from school. I wrote a poem in my head and then I wrote it down, and after that writing was the only thing I wanted to do.' She has published thirteen poetry collections, including a *Selected Poems* and *Selected Poems II*. Her novels include *Cat's Eye, Alias Grace* and *The Blind Assassin*.

Sara BERKELEY was born in Dublin in 1967 and now lives in California, where she works as a computer analyst. She published her first collection, *Penn*, when she was nineteen. Bloodaxe Books published *Facts About Water* (new and selected poems) in 1994. She has also published a collection of short stories, *The Swimmer in the Deep Blue Dream*, and a novel, *Shadowing Hannah*.

Rosita BOLAND was born in County Clare in 1965 and published her first collection, *Muscle Creek*, in 1991. She works for *The Irish Times*.

Pat BORAN was born in Portlaoise in 1963 and now lives in Dublin. He has published four collections to date: *The Unwound Clock, Familiar Things, The Shape of Water* and *As the Hand the Glove*. He is Programme Director of the Dublin Writers Festival. His other works include *The Portable Creative Writing Workshop* and *A Short History of Dublin*.

Colette BRYCE was born in Derry in 1970. She 'grew up as the war grew up and it was a big part of my life'. She left Ireland at eighteen and now lives in London. Her first collection, *The Heel of Bernadette*, was published in 2000.

Billy COLLINS is the US Poet Laureate and Professor of English at Lehman College, CUNY, and for several years conducted summer poetry workshops at NUI Galway. He was born in New York City in 1941. His books include *The Art of Drowning, Questions About Angels, Picnic, Lightning* and *Taking Off Emily Dickinson's Clothes*.

Wendy COPE was born in Kent in 1945 and is a best-selling poet. Her collections include *Making Cocoa for Kingsley Amis, Serious Concerns* and *If I Don't Know*.

Gregory CORSO was born in New York City in 1930 and, with Allen Ginsberg and Jack Kerouac, was one of the original Beats. His collection of new and selected poems is called *Mindfield*.

E. E. CUMMINGS was born in Cambridge, Massachusetts, in 1894. His poetry is typographically distinctive and his first collection, *Tulips and Chimneys* was very popular. Other collections include *No Thanks* and *Xaipe*. He died in 1962. The 'E. E.' stands for Edward Estlin.

Greg DELANTY was born in Cork in 1958. He won the Patrick Kavanagh Award with his first collection, *Cast in the Fire*. Other collections include *Southward, American Wake, The Hellbox* and *The Blind Stitch*. He lives in Burlington, Vermont.

John DOLAN lives in Dunedin, New Zealand, where he is senior lecturer in the English Department at the University of Otago. He published his collection *Stuck Up* in 1995. He says that 'the disjunction between violent, romantic, nerdy imagination and cool, ironical, suburban setting is at the heart of my poetry.'

Carol Ann DUFFY was born in Glasgow in 1955 and grew up in England. She studied philosophy at Liverpool University and now teaches at Manchester Metropolitan University. Her collections include *Standing Female Nude, Selling Manhattan, The Other Country, Mean Time, Selected Poems, The World's Wife* and *Feminine Gospels*.

Paul DURCAN was born in Dublin in 1944 and has published over fifteen collections, including *The Berlin Wall Café, Going Home to Russia, Greetings to Our Friends in Brazil* and *Cries of an Irish Caveman*.

D. J. ENRIGHT was born in 1920, was educated at Cambridge and the University of Alexandria and spent many years teaching in Egypt, Japan, Thailand and Singapore. His *Collected Poems* was published in 1987.

Peter FALLON was born in Germany in 1951 and grew up in County Meath, where he now lives. He founded the Gallery Press at eighteen and has published over three hundred titles under that imprint. His *News of the World, Selected and New Poems* was published in 1978.

Paul FARLEY was born in Liverpool in 1965 and studied at the Chelsea School of Art. His first collection, *The Boy from the Chemist Is Here to See You* (1998), won a Forward Prize for Best First Collection and he was named Sunday Times Young Writer of the Year. His second collection, *The Ice Age*, was published in 2002.

Lawrence FERLINGHETTI was born in Yonkers, New York, but is associated with the Bay Area and San Francisco, where he founded the City Lights publishing house and bookstore. His *A Coney Island of the Mind* was published in 1958 and was one of the big poetry best-sellers of the twentieth century. *Endless Life: Selected Poems* was published in 1981.

Tom FRENCH was born in Kilkenny in 1966. He published his first collection, *Touching the Bones,* in 2001. Having worked in Spain, France and the US, he now lives in Dublin and works in the library service in County Wicklow.

Patrick GALVIN was born in 1927 in Cork City and left school early, having had his birth certificate altered. He subsequently worked as a messenger boy, newspaper boy and assistant film projectionist. He joined the RAF and later lived on an Israeli kibbutz and in London. He published his first collection, *Heart of*

Grace, in 1957. Other collections include *Christ in London* and *The Woodburners.* A *New and Selected Poems* was published in 1996. He has also written plays and two volumes of autobiography.

Michael GORMAN was born in Sligo in 1952. He has published three collections: *Postcards from Galway* (1980), *Waiting for the Sky to Fall* (1984) and *Up She Flew* (1991).

Mark GRANIER published his first collection, *Airborne,* in 2001.

Jack GRAPES likes his own poems. His 'I Like My Own Poems' is from his collection *Trees, Coffee, and the Eyes of Deer,* published by Bombshelter Press in 1987.

Lavinia GREENLAW was born in London in 1962. She has worked in publishing and arts administration, and is now a freelance writer. She has published two collections, *Night Photographs* and *A World Where News Travelled Slowly*, and her novel, *Mary George of Allnorthover*, was published in 2001.

Vona GROARKE was born in Edgeworthstown, County Longford, in 1964 and now lives in Dundalk. She has published three collections: *Shale* (1994), *Other People's Houses* (1999) and *Flight* (2002).

Thom GUNN (the 'Thom' is for 'Thompson') was born in Gravesend, England, in 1929 but has lived in America since 1954. He settled in San Francisco in 1961 and taught at the University of California at Berkeley. His *Collected Poems* was published in 1993.

Anne HAVERTY was born in Tipperary in 1959. She has written a biography of Constance Markievicz and two novels: *One Day as a Tiger* (winner of the 1997 Rooney Prize) and *The Far Side of a Kiss*. In 1999 she published a collection of poetry, *The Beauty of the Moon*. She is a member of Aosdána.

Dermot HEALY was born in Finea, County Westmeath, in 1947. He has written short stories, novels, plays and a memoir and has published three poetry collections: *The Ballyconnell Colours, What the Hammer* and *The Reed Bed.*

Seamus HEANEY was born in County Derry in 1939. By 1998, when *Opened Ground: Poems 1966–1996* was published, his poetry was known and read worldwide. *Finders Keepers: Selected Prose 1971–2001* was published in 2002.

Rita Ann HIGGINS was born in Galway in 1955. She did not complete formal schooling but read widely and studied at the university of life. Her collections include *Goddess on the Mervue Bus* (1986), *Witch in the Bushes* (1988), *Goddess & Witch* (1990), *Philomena's Revenge* (1992), *Higher Purchase* (1996) and *An Awful Racket* (2001).

Joseph HORGAN was born in Birmingham of Irish parents and now lives in County Cork. He is a columnist with the *Irish Post* and has had poems published in *The Stinging Fly, THE SHOp, Poetry Ireland Review, Books Ireland, Staple* and *Poetry Birmingham.*

Pearse HUTCHINSON was born in Glasgow in 1927; he and his Irish parents moved to Dublin in 1932. He lived abroad for several years and has written in Irish and English. His *Collected Poems* was published in 2002.

Trevor JOYCE was born in 1947 and grew up in Dublin and the Galway Gaeltacht. He co-founded the New Writers' Press in 1967, studied Philosophy and Mathematical Science and has lectured on Chinese poetry. He lives in Cork. *With the First Dream of Fire They Hunt the Cold*, his most recent book, gathers together a body of work from 1966 to 2000.

Rita KELLY was born in east Galway in 1953 and writes poetry and fiction in Irish and English. Poetry collections include *Fare Well – Beir Beannacht* and *Travelling West*. A collaboration with Pauline Bewick, *Kelly Reads Bewick,* a response to the artist's work, was published in 2001.

Brendan KENNELLY was born in Ballylongford, County Kerry, in 1936, and was appointed Professor of Modern Literature at Trinity College in 1973. His poetry collections include *The Book of Judas, Poetry My Arse* and *The Man Made of Rain*. He is also a translator, editor and anthologist.

August KLEINZAHLER was born in Jersey City, New Jersey, in 1949 and now lives in San Francisco. His collections include *Storm Over Hackensack; Earthquake Weather; Like Cities, Like Storms; Red Sauce, Whiskey and Snow;* and *Green Sees Things in Waves*. Allen Ginsberg called him 'a loner, a genius'.

Christopher LOGUE was born in 1926. He served in the British Army between 1944 and 1948 and was imprisoned for sixteen months. His first collection, *Wand and Quadrant,* was published in 1953. Ezra Pound said of it: 'Not bad. I can read quite a bit of it.' He has published over thirty books, including a pornographic novel and *Ode to the Dodo: Poems from 1953 to 1978*.

Catherine Phil MacCARTHY was born in 1954 and grew up in County Limerick. She has published two collections: *This Hour of the Tide* (1994) and *The Blue Globe* (1998).

Iggy McGOVERN teaches Physics at Trinity College Dublin and received the Hennessy Award for Poetry in 2001.

Aidan MATHEWS is a novelist *(Muesli at Midnight)*, short-story writer *(Adventures in a Bathyscope; Lipstick on the Host)*, playwright *(Exit/Entrance; Communion)* and poet. He was born in Dublin in 1956 and works in the Drama Department of RTÉ Radio. His three poetry collections are *Windfalls*, *Minding Ruth* and *According to the Small Hours*.

Adrian MITCHELL was born in London in 1932 and has written poetry, plays and several collections of stories and poems for children. He is more interested in performance than print and his most important books are *For Beauty Douglas: Adrian Mitchell's Collected Poems 1953–1979* and *Blue Coffee Poems 1985–1996*.

Noel MONAGHAN was born in Granard, County Longford, and now lives in Cavan. He has published three poetry collections: *Opposite Walls, Snowfire* and *Curse of the Birds*. He has also written plays and won first prize in the *Poetry Ireland*/Seacat Poetry Competition 2001.

Edwin MORGAN was born in 1920 in Glasgow and later became a professor at Glasgow University. A *Collected Poems* was published in 1990.

Thylias MOSS, an African-American, was born in 1954 and studied at Oberlin College and the University of New Hampshire. Her poetry was featured in *The United States of Poetry* and her 1991 collection, *Rainbow Remnants in Rock Bottom Ghetto Sky*, was a National Poetry Series Award winner.

Andrew MOTION was born in London in 1952. He studied at Oxford and taught at Hull. He published his first collection, *The Pleasure Steamers*, in 1978. A *Selected Poems* was published in 1998. He was named Britain's Poet Laureate in May 1999.

Paul MULDOON was born in Portadown, County Armagh, in 1951. He now lives in the US, where he is a professor at Princeton University. His first collection, *New Weather,* was published when he was twenty-one and a *New and Selected Poems* was published in 1996.

Julie O'CALLAGHAN was born in Chicago in 1954 and now lives in Naas. She has published two collections for younger readers, *Taking my Pen for a Walk* and *Two Barks.* She has also published *Edible Anecdotes, What's What* and *No Can Do.*

Philip O'CEALLAIGH won the Hennessy Award for prose in 1998 and, in 2001, the Hennessy Award for Poetry. He also received an Arts Council Bursary. He lives in Bucharest, Romania.

Mary O'DONOGHUE was born in County Clare. Her first collection, *Tulle,* was published in 2001 and she was named Writer of the Year in the *Sunday Tribune*/Hennessy Awards.

Dennis O'DRISCOLL was born in Thurles in 1954 and works in the head office of Irish Customs in Dublin. He has published five collections: *Kist, Hidden Extras, Long Short Story, Quality Time* and *Weather Permitting. Troubled Thoughts, Majestic Dreams* is a collection of his selected prose writings.

Frank O'HARA was born in Maryland in 1926. He studied music, then English, at Harvard and worked at the New York Museum of Modern Art. He published his first book of poems at twenty-six and died in 1966 as a result of having been struck by a beach buggy on Fire Island. There is a *Collected Poems.*

Caitríona O'REILLY was born in Dublin in 1973 and has written a doctoral thesis on American literature. She published her first collection, *The Nowhere Birds*, in 2001. It was described by Michael Longley as 'a stunning debut collection'. She was awarded the 2002 Rooney Prize.

Linda PASTAN was born in 1932, grew up in New York and lives in Washington DC. Collections include *A Fraction of Darkness* and *The Imperfect Paradise*. There is also a *New and Selected Poems* (1982).

Don PATERSON was born in Dundee in 1963. He left school at sixteen and has worked as a professional jazz musician and writer-in-residence. His *Nil Nil* won the Forward Prize for best first collection and his poem 'A Private Bottling' won first prize in the Arvon Poetry Competition. His second collection, *God's Gift to Women*, was published in 1997.

Tom PAULIN, poet, academic and outspoken and controversial commentator, was born in Leeds in 1949 and grew up in Belfast. His poetry books include *A State of Justice, Liberty Tree, Fivemiletown* and *The Invasion Handbook*. He also edited *The Faber Book of Political Verse*.

Harold PINTER was born in London in 1930 and is best known as a playwright *(The Birthday Party, The Caretaker, The Homecoming)*. His *Collected Poems and Prose* was published in 1986.

Tom POW was born in Edinburgh in 1950, has taught in Edinburgh, London and Madrid and now teaches at the University of Glasgow at Dumfries. His poetry collections include *Rough Seas* (1987), *The Moth Trap* (1990) and *Red Letter Day* (1996). He has also written plays for radio, and the travel book *In the Palace of Serpents: An Experience of Peru*.

Justin QUINN was born in Dublin in 1968 and graduated from Trinity College. He now teaches at the Charles University in Prague and is an editor of *Metre*. He has published two collections, *The 'O'o'a'a' Bird* and *Privacy*.

Peter READING was born in Liverpool in 1946 and has worked as a teacher, lecturer in art history and weighbridge operator. His collections include *Stet, Shitheads: New Poems* and his two volumes of *Collected Poems*.

Robin ROBERTSON was born in Scotland in 1955. He studied there and in Canada before moving to London where he now works as a senior editorial director at Jonathan Cape. His first collection, *A Painted Field*, won the Forward Poetry Prize in 1997 and his second collection, *Slow Air*, was published in 2002.

Nicholas SANZ-GOULD was six or seven years old in the summer of 1996 when he won a prize for his poem 'Sad Sun'. He read the poem at a Poetry Festival in San Francisco and was introduced by Lawrence Ferlinghetti.

Henry SHUKMAN won first prize in *The Daily Telegraph*/Arvon International Poetry Competition in 2000. More than 8,000 poems were submitted for the contest, which was judged by Carol Ann Duffy, Simon Armitage and Allison Pearson.

Charles SIMIC was born in Yugoslavia in 1938 and emigrated with his family to the US when he was eleven. His first book was *Dismantling the Silence* (1971) and he has published several other volumes, including *Unending Blues, The World Doesn't End* and *The Book of Gods and Devils*. There is also a *Selected Poems*.

Mark STRAND was born on Prince Edward Island, Canada in 1934. His studies included literature and painting and he is now director of the Creative Writing Program at the University of Utah. His *Selected Poems* was published in 1980.

Jean VALENTINE was born in Chicago in 1934 and now lives in New York. She has published several collections, and a selected poems, *The Under Voice,* was published by 1995.

Eamonn WALL has published two collections, *Dyckman – 200 Street* (1994) and *Iron Mountain Road* (1997). He lives in the US.

Tom WAYMAN was born in 1945. He has had poetry published in *The Norton Introduction to Poetry.*

David WHEATLEY was born in Dublin in 1970 and was awarded the Rooney Prize for Irish Literature for his first collection, *Thirst.* His second collection, *Misery Hill,* was published in 2000. He is a founder editor of *Metre* and lectures at the University of Hull.

Hugo WILLIAMS was born at Windsor in 1942 and educated at Eton. After school he worked for the *London Magazine* and then, aged twenty, spent twenty months travelling around the world. In 1989 he published his *Selected Poems*. His poem 'Toilet' was voted 89th in Britain's *The Nation's Favourite Poems.*

William Carlos WILLIAMS was born in Rutherford, New Jersey, in 1883. He studied medicine and worked as a GP. He was later appointed head paediatrician at Paterson General Hospital. He published his first book of poems, *The Tempers,* in 1913. The *Collected Poems,* in two volumes, was published in 1986 and 1988.

Franz WRIGHT has had poems published in *The New Yorker.*

INDEX OF FIRST LINES

Leabharlanna Poibli Chathair Baile Átha Cliath

Dublin City Public Libraries

Index of Titles

INDEX OF POETS

COPYRIGHT PERMISSIONS

Every effort has been made to get in touch with copyright holders. The publishers would be grateful to be notified of any errors or omissions in the list below and will be happy to make good any such errors or omissions in future printings.

'Coupling', 'Roles' and 'The Video' by Fleur Adcock from *Poems 1960–2000*, Bloodaxe Books, 2000; 'On the Amtrak from Boston to New York City' reprinted from *First Indian on the Moon* ©1993 by Sherman Alexie, by permission of Hanging Loose Press; Simon Armitage for 'The Shout'; Faber and Faber for 'Hitcher' from *Book of Matches* by Simon Armitage; Little, Brown and Company for 'They Eat Out' by Margaret Atwood; Sara Berkeley for 'Burying the Elephant'; Rosita Boland for 'A Severed Leg', 'World Expo, Brisbane' and 'Lipstick'; 'Seven Things Nature Did in the Last Five Minutes', 'Seven Things Wasted on Lovers' and 'Seven Unpopular Things to Say about Blood' by Pat Boran from *Familiar Things*, The Dedalus Press; 'Epilogue' by Colette Bryce from *The Heel of Bernadette* (Macmillan); 'Going Out for Cigarettes', 'Marginalia', and 'Walking Across the Atlantic' by Billy Collins from *Taking Off Emily Dickinson's Clothes* (Macmillan); Faber and Faber for 'Song' from *If I Don't Know* by Wendy Cope and 'The Uncertainty of the Poet from *Serious Concerns* by Wendy Cope; 'The Whole Mess, Almost' by Gregory Corso, from *Herald of the Autochthonic Spirit*, copyright ©1973, 1975, 1981 by Gregory Corso, reprinted by permission of New Directions Publishing Corp.; 'may i feel said he' is reprinted from *Complete Poems 1904–1962* by E. E. Cummings, edited by George J. Firmage, by permission of W. W. Norton & Company, copyright © 1991 by the Trustees for the E. E. Cummings Trust and George James Firmage; 'The Night's Takings' by Gerald Dawe, by kind permission of the author and The Gallery Press, Loughcrew, Oldcastle, County Meath, Ireland; 'The Seahorse Family' from *The Morning Train* (1999) by Greg Delanty, by permission of the author and Carcanet Press Limited; John Dolan and Auckland University Press for 'The Wordsworth Goes on a Journey'; 'Two Small Poems of Desire' is taken from *The Other Country* by Carol Ann Duffy, published by Anvil Press Poetry in 1990; 'The Cabinet Table' from *A Snail in My Prime* © Paul Durcan, 1993, reproduced by permission of the Harvill Press; 'Country Music' by Peter Fallon by kind permission of the author and the Gallery Press, Loughcrew, Oldcastle, County Meath, Ireland, from *News of the World* (1998); Macmillan for 'Jingle' and 'Treacle' from *The Boy from the Chemist Is Here to See You* by Paul Farley; 'Sometime During Eternity' by Lawrence Ferlinghetti, from *A Coney Island of the Mind,* copyright ©1958 by Lawrence Ferlinghetti, reprinted by permission of New Directions Publishing Corp.; 'Two Scavengers in a Truck, Two Beautiful People in a Mercedes' by Lawrence Ferlinghetti, from *These Are My Rivers,* copyright ©1979 by Lawrence Ferlinghetti, reprinted by permission of New Directions Publishing Corp.; 'Ghost Ship' by Tom French, by kind permission of the author and the Gallery Press, Loughcrew, Oldcastle, County Meath, from *Touching the Bones* (2001); 'The Perfect Bar of Soap' and 'Advice to a Poet', copyright © Patrick Galvin 1996 from *New and Selected Poems of Patrick Galvin* edited by Greg Delanty and Robert Welch, reproduced by kind permission of the author c/o Cork University Press, Crawford Business Park, Crosses Green, Cork, Ireland; 'She Elopes with Marc Chagall' from Michael Gorman, *Up She Flew* (Salmon Publishing, 1991); 'The Instrument', '7Up, Torremolinos', and 'Holding Pattern, Dún Aengus' from *Airborne* by Mark Granier (County Clare: Salmon Publishing, 2001); Faber and Faber for 'The Gift of Life' from *Night Photograph* by Lavinia Greenlaw; 'World Music' from *Flight* (2002) by Vona Groarke, by kind permission of the author and The Gallery Press, Loughcrew, Oldcastle, County Meath, Ireland; Faber and Faber for 'Courage, a Tale' from *Jack Straw's Castle* by Thom Gunn; Tony Harrison for 'Timer'; 'The Bag Ladies' and 'In the Country' from *The Beauty of the Moon* by Anne Haverty, published by Chatto & Windus, used by permission of The Random House Group Limited; 'One

Minute with Eileen' and 'The Wall I Built' from *The Reed Bed* (2001) by Dermot Healy by kind permission of the author and The Gallery Press, Loughcrew, Oldcastle, County Meath, Ireland; Faber and Faber for 'Widgeon' from *Station Island* by Seamus Heaney; 'Lucky Mrs Higgins' and 'The Visionary' by Rita Ann Higgins from *An Awful Racket*, Bloodaxe Books, 2000; Joe Horgan for 'The Act'; 'Findrum', 'Nár Mhéanar É' and 'Wouldn't It Be Lovely' by Pearse Hutchinson by kind permission of the author and The Gallery Press, Loughcrew, Oldcastle, County Meath, Ireland; New Writers' Press for 'An Execution Remembered' by Trevor Joyce from *with the first dream of fire they hunt the cold*; 'Fan', 'Zany Rain' and 'To No One' by Brendan Kennelly from *Poetry My Arse*, Bloodaxe Books, 1995; Faber and Faber for 'Green Sees Things in Waves' from *Green Sees Things in Waves* by August Kleinzahler; Faber and Faber for 'Madam' from *Selected Poems* by Christopher Logue; Blackstaff Press for 'The Show' from *The Blue Globe* by Catherine Phil MacCarthy; Iggy McGovern for 'Eirata' and 'On Not Winning the Kavanagh Award for the Umpteenth Time'; Aidan Mathews for 'At the Junction' and 'Decency'; Adrian Mitchell for 'Celia, Celia' from *For Beauty Douglas* (Bloodaxe Books); 'In School' and 'Donnelly's Bus' from Noel Monaghan, *Curse of the Birds* (County Clare: Salmon Publishing, 2000); Carcanet Press for 'The Video Box: 25' from *Collected Poems* by Edwin Morgan; Faber and Faber for 'It Is an Offence' from *Selected Poems* by Andrew Motion; Faber and Faber for 'The Briefcase' from *Selected Poems* by Paul Muldoon; Julie O'Callaghan for 'What I Saw' from *Edible Anecdotes*, Dolmen Press, 1983; 'Adios', 'The Great Blasket Island', 'Pep-Talk to Poets from Their Sales Manager', 'Saturday Afternoon in Dublin' from *What's What*, Bloodaxe Books, 1991; Philip O'Ceallaigh for 'The Bridge'; 'Widening the Canal', 'Edict' and 'The Witches of Móinín na gCloigeann' from Mary O'Donoghue, *Tulle* (County Clare: Salmon Publishing, 2001); 'Nor' and 'Buying a Letterbox' are taken from *Weather Permitting* by Dennis O'Driscoll, published by Anvil Press Poetry in 1999; 'Poem' and 'Why I Am Not a Painter' from *Selected Poems* by Frank O'Hara by permission of the author and Carcanet Press Limited; 'Nineteen Eighty-Four' and 'Six' by Caitríona O'Reilly from *The Nowhere Birds*, Bloodaxe Books, 2001; 'Marks', from *The Five Stages of Grief* by Linda Pastan. Copyright © 1978 by Linda Pastan. Used by permission of W. W. Norton & Company, Inc.; Faber and Faber for 'Postmodern' from *God's Gift to Women* by Don Paterson; Faber and Faber for 'Painting with Sawdust' from *The Liberty Tree* by Tom Paulin; Faber and Faber for 'Message' from *Various Voices* by Harold Pinter; Tom Pow for 'A Brief History of Your Breasts'; 'Hoover' from *Six Household Appliances* by Justin Quinn by permission of the author and Carcanet Press Limited; 'Autumn Evening' from *Privacy* by Justin Quinn by permission of the author and Carcanet Press Limited; '10 x 10 x 10' by Peter Reading from *Collected Poems, v. 1*, Bloodaxe Books, 1995; 'Shakespearean' by Peter Reading from *Work in Regress*, Bloodaxe Books, 1997; Macmillan for 'Break' and 'Anxiety #5' from *Slow Air* by Robin Robertson; Faber and Faber for 'Watermelons' from *Looking for Trouble* by Charles Simic; '3 A.M. in New York' by Jean Valentine from *The Under Voice* (Salmon Publishing, 1995); 'Belongings with Attitude' by Eamonn Wall from *Iron Mountain Road* (Salmon Publishing, 1997; reprinted 1999); Harbour Publishing for 'Wayman in Love' by Tom Wayman; 'Traffic' by David Wheatley, by kind permission of the author and The Gallery Press, Loughcrew, Oldcastle, County Meath, Ireland. From *Misery Hill* (2000); 'Danse Russe' from *Collected Poems* by William Carlos Williams by permission of the author and Carcanet Press Limited.

ACKNOWLEDGEMENTS

Thanks to Mary Clayton, Rolly Dingle, Marybeth Joyce, Riona MacMonagle, James Hanley, Kate Bateman, Lindi Dingle, Faith O'Grady, Janet Wilson, Joan McBreen, Noel Duffy; and to the marvellous Marino team – Jo O'Donoghue, Claire McVeigh, Caitríona Bennett, Robert Doran, Seán O'Keeffe and especially Jane Casey.

REAL COOL
POEMS TO GROW UP WITH

EDITED BY
NIALL MACMONAGLE

This upbeat and original bestselling anthology gathers together poems by Irish and international poets of the first rank. Guaranteed to appeal to young people and even, perhaps, to throw light on some of the shadows of troubled adolescent years, the anthology features work by poets such as Sharon Olds, Paul Durcan, Rita Ann Higgins, Adrienne Rich, Derek Mahon, Seamus Heaney, Carol Ann Duffy, Paula Meehan, Simon Armitage, Fleur Adcock, Robert Frost, Eavan Boland, Brian Patten, Elizabeth Bishop, Paul Muldoon, Wendy Cope, Peter Reading and Brendan Kennelly . . .

PRAISE FOR REAL COOL

'For young and new readers certainly; for poetry lovers an absolute must.'

RTÉ Guide

'A stunning anthology'

Robert Dunbar
Children's Literature Association of Ireland

'I can only think of three outstanding anthologies. *Real Cool* joins that short list.'

John Boland

'A wonderfully eclectic and entertaining selection. Heartily recommended.'

The Irish Times

'This is a collection, not just to grow up with, but to live with.'

Pat Donlon

'*Real Cool* is an anthology which breaks the traditional mould. But it does so in a way which gives credence to the past for its glories, and then offers a substantial and generally impressive body of poetry which should remain of lasting interest to young people.'

Tom Mullins
The Big Guide to Irish Children's Books

OUTSIDE IN
STORIES TO GROW UP WITH

EDITED BY
NIALL MACMONAGLE

Here are twenty contemporary short stories that deal with life's joys and troubles. This wide-ranging and stimulating collection is sure to appeal to young people. Love and loss, adventure and reflection – all are explored in this superb anthology.

Authors include Alice Munro, William Trevor, Lorrie Moore, Mary O'Donnell, Tim O'Brien, John McGahern, Muriel Spark, Aidan Mathews, Eilís Ní Dhuibhne, Joseph O'Connor, Colum McCann and Anne Enright – writers from Ireland and around the world.

Praise for Outside In

'The teacher who anthologised the poems teenagers could really relate to *(Real Cool)* has done well or better with twenty modern short stories . . . it's a book that will open doors and windows for many young people.'

Books Ireland

'The bedroom light never gets put out with these tales – a present to please parents as well as the young reader.'

Irish Examiner

'This unusual book will capture the imagination and hold the interest of adolescents everywhere.'

Ali Henderson

SLOW TIME
100 POEMS TO TAKE YOU THERE

EDITED BY
NIALL MACMONAGLE

This collection brings together relaxing, inspiring and meditative verse from leading Irish and international poets. The poems provide a commentary on the personal and yet universally felt experiences that shape our lives: love, death, laughter and sorrow, childhood and old age, the past and the future.

Slow Time features poems such as 'Love after Love' by Derek Walcott, 'Elegy for a Still-born Child' by Seamus Heaney, 'On Finding an Old Photograph' by Wendy Cope, 'A Summer Night' by W.H. Auden, 'The Trees' by Philip Larkin and 'Nocturne' by Eavan Boland.

PRAISE FOR SLOW TIME

'An anthology to feed the soul, chosen by the best-known English teacher in the country. MacMonagle's *Real Cool* was one of the truly innovative poetry selections of recent years: here he proposes time out for more mature readers with more good things from contemporary poets, Irish and international . . . Nothing ordinary here.

Mary Finn
RTÉ Guide

'These poems stay with you to become familiar friends'

Mayo News